2nd edition

Korean made easy **for beginners**

Korean made easy for beginners   2nd edition

Written by   Seung-eun Oh
Translated by   Jennifer Lee, Isabel Kim Dzitac
Illustrated by   Moon-su Kim, Byung-chul Yoon

First Published   March, 2006
Second Edition   July, 2021
3rd Printing   July, 2023
Publisher   Kyu-do Chung
Editor   Suk-hee Lee, Jihee Han, Mi-sook Kim, Hye-won Park
Designer   Na-kyoung Kim, Hyun-seok Jung, Dae-hun Kwon,
                 Eun-bi Park
Voice Actor   So-yun Shin, Rae-whan Kim, Toosix Media

월 DARAKWON Published by Darakwon Inc.

Darakwon Bldg., 211, Munbal-ro, Paju-si, Gyeonggi-do
Republic of Korea 10881
Tel : 82-2-736-2031
(Marketing Dept. ext.: 250~252　Editorial Dept. ext.: 420~426)
Fax : 82-2-732-2037

ISBN : 978-89-277-3273-0　14710
         978-89-277-3272-3 (set)

http://www.darakwon.co.kr
http://koreanbooks.darakwon.co.kr

※ Visit the Darakwon homepage to learn about our other publications and promotions, and
to download the contents of MP3 format.

Seung-eun Oh

Preface

〈Korean Made Easy〉 시리즈는 제2언어 혹은 외국어로서 한국어를 공부하는 학습자를 위해 집필되었다. 특히 이 책은 시간적·공간적 제약으로 인해 정규 한국어 교육을 받을 수 없었던 학습자를 위해 혼자서도 한국어를 공부할 수 있도록 기획되었다. 〈Korean Made Easy〉 시리즈는 초판 발행 이후 오랜 시간 독자의 사랑과 지지를 받으며 전세계 다양한 언어로 번역되어 한국어 학습에 길잡이 역할을 했다고 생각한다. 이번에 최신 문화를 반영하여 예문을 깁고 연습 문제를 보완하여 개정판을 출판하게 되어 저자로서 크나큰 보람을 느낀다. 한국어를 공부하려는 모든 학습자가 〈Korean Made Easy〉를 통해 효과적으로 한국어를 공부하면서 즐길 수 있기를 바란다.

시리즈 중 〈Korean Made Easy for Beginners〉는 한국어를 처음 접하는 학습자가 좀더 쉽고 재미있게 한국어를 학습하도록 고안되었다. 어렵고 딱딱한 문법 설명보다는 기초적이고 핵심적인 문법 설명을 제공하고 모든 학습 내용을 시각 자료로 제시함으로써 학습자가 언어 사용 맥락을 쉽게 이해하며 따라가도록 하였다. 그리고 도움말과 부록으로 보충 설명을 더하여 학습자가 교사 없이도 초급 한국어를 익힐 수 있도록 하였다. 또한 간결한 대화와 실용 표현, 초급 문형 별책을 통해 학습자가 일상생활에서 생존에 필요한 한국어를 구사할 수 있도록 하였다.

〈Korean Made Easy for Beginners〉는 크게 한글 네 과와 본문 스무 과, 별책으로 구성되어 있다. 한글은 시청각 자료와 듣기 연습 문제를 통해 한글 구성과 발음을 체계적으로 익힐 수 있다. 본문은 일상생활에서 필수적인 40 개의 주제·상황을 다양하게 접할 수 있는데, 초급 어휘와 문법을 단계적으로 학습하고 대화와 실용 표현으로 다양한 상황에서 어휘와 문법이 쓰이는 맥락을 확인할 수 있다. 각 과의 마지막에 실려 있는 문화 정보로 한국 문화에 대한 이해도 높일 수 있다. 별책은 본문에 나온 초급 핵심 문형 40개를 모아 놓은 것으로, 실제 생활에서 학습자는 별책을 이용하여 책에서 배운 한국어를 바로 사용할 수 있다.

이 책을 집필하는 데 많은 이의 관심과 도움이 있었다. 먼저, 이 책의 큰 틀을 잡고 방향을 설정하는 데 도움을 주신 고(故)김성희 선생님과 세부적인 내용을 꼼꼼하게 지적해 주신 오승민 선생님과 김은정 선생님께 감사드린다. 한국어 학습 경험을 바탕으로 쉽고 명확한 번역을 해 주신 번역자 Jennifer Lee께 감사드린다. 그리고 초판에서 문법과 발음은 Stephanie Speirs, 한글 발음은 Bonnie Tilland, 문화는 Esther Cho가 도움을 주었고 책의 마무리 단계에서 박석영과 Christopher Barnes가 조언해 주었다. 초판의 영어 교정에서 Tyler Lau와 Eugene Lee, 개정판의 영어 번역에서 Isabel Kim Dzitac이 함께하여 이 책이 독자에게 자연스러운 영어로 다가갈 수 있었다. 이분들의 참여와 열정으로 책의 완성도를 높일 수 있었다. 이 모든 분들께 다시 한번 깊은 감사를 드린다.

또한 지난한 출판 작업 중에서도 인내심을 갖고 기다려 주신 ㈜다락원의 고(故) 정효섭 회장님과 정규도 사장님, 더 좋은 책이 되도록 많은 애를 써 주신 편집부와 디자이너께도 감사 인사를 드린다. 마지막으로, 딸의 원고 작업을 곁에서 지켜보며 항상 기도해 주시는 어머니와 딸의 작업을 지지해 주셨던 고인이 되신 아버님께 감사드리고 싶다.

오승은

The *Korean Made Easy* series was written for non-native Korean language learners. In particular, this book was designed for learners who cannot receive regular Korean language education. The *Korean Made Easy* series has been loved and supported by readers for a long time since its first edition. It has since been translated into various languages around the world and has served as a guide to those learning Korean. I feel rewarded as an author, as the revised version offers supplemental exercises that incorporate example sentences reflecting the culture of the present. I hope that all learners who want to study Korean can study Korean effectively and enjoyably through *Korean Made Easy*.

Among the series, *Korean Made Easy for Beginners* is designed to make learning Korean easier and more enjoyable for learners who are new to Korean. Rather than difficult and hard-to-understand grammar explanations, basic and core grammar explanations are provided. All learning contents are presented visually so that learners can easily understand and follow the context of language use. In addition, in hopes that learners can learn elementary Korean without a teacher, supplementary explanations can be found in the help boxes or appendix. Furthermore, concise conversations, useful phrases, and a key phrase book enable beginner learners to speak survival Korean in everyday life.

Korean Made Easy for Beginners is composed of four Hangeul chapters, twenty chapters in the main text, and a key phrase book. In the Hangeul chapters, one can systematically discover the composition and pronunciation of Hangeul through audiovisual materials and listening exercises. The main text is composed of forty topics and situations essential in everyday life in various ways. You can learn elementary vocabulary and grammar step by step, and check the context in which vocabulary and grammar are used in diverse situations through conversations and useful expressions. You can also increase your understanding of Korean culture with information found at the end of each chapter. The key phrase book comprises of forty basic sentence patterns from the main text. The learner can use the Korean language learned from the book in real life by making use of a key phrase book.

There was a lot of interest and help in the writing of this book. First of all, I would like to thank the late Sung-hee Kim and Seung-min Oh and Eun-jung Kim for their attention to detail. Thanks to the translator Jennifer Lee for making clear and easy-to understand translations based on her Korean learning experience. In the first edition, I would like to thank Stephanie Speirs for her close eye to grammar and pronunciation, Bonnie Tilland for her attention to Korean pronunciation, Esther Cho for assisting with the cultural aspects, and Seok-young Park and Christopher Barnes for offering advice during the completion stage of this book. This book was able to reach the reader in natural English thanks to the assistance of Tyler Lau and Eugene Lee in the first edition and Isabel Kim Dzitac in the revised English translation. It is thanks to their participation and enthusiasm that I was able to improve the quality of this book. Once again, I would like to express gratitude to all of these people.

In addition, I would like to express my gratitude to the late Chairman Hyo-seop Chung and President Kyu-do Chung of Darakwon Co., Ltd. for patiently waiting for the last publication work, and the editorial department and designers who have worked hard in the making of a better book. Lastly, I would like to thank my mother who always prayed and looked over the manuscript, and my belated father who supported my work.

Seung-eun Oh

How to use this book

Hangeul | Hangeul is divided into the introduction and four chapters, with the consonants and vowels grouped together by their unique characteristics, in order to make them easy to learn and read.

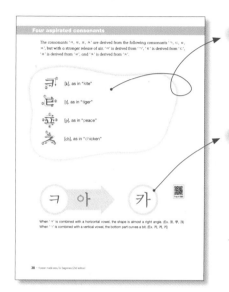

Presentation of Learning Objectives

This chapter shows the method of writing Hangeul, the pronunciation of each consonant and vowel, and some English pronunciations similar to those of Korean.

Pronunciation with Audio

The character in the left circle shows a learning objective and the character in the arrow shows the syllable that has been learned. When these two characters are combined, a syllable is formed as in the right circle. You will hear each chapter once from the arrow and right circle, respectively through the QR code's audio.

Vocabulary

Each character taught from the section is combined to present different vocabulary. As an aid, the vocabulary is presented with pictures. You will hear each word twice from the audio through the QR code.

Be Careful!

This section is organized to make it easier for learners to study by showing the differences in pronunciation of words that look similar or by checking the different spellings that are pronounced with the same sound more clearly. You can hear the pronunciation through the audio via the QR code.

Main Text

The main part of this book is separated into twenty different chapters, each with complementary topics and grammar lessons. As the main purpose of this book is to teach grammar, the book covers the most frequently-used grammatical patterns first.

▶ *Key Sentences & Grammar* : This section introduces new grammar with a topic sentence.

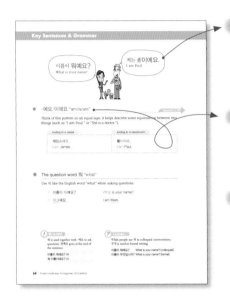

Chapter Topic

The purpose of each chapter is described in a picture with various phrases that provide the learner with appropriate usages and situations in which these patterns can be incorporated in different sentences.

Grammar Explanation

The grammar is explained in a simple manner, presented visually with easy to understand examples.

Be Careful!

This section calls attention to common mistakes and pitfalls.

I Wonder...

This section highlights difficult concepts and exceptions.

▶ *Conversation* : The conversation section introduces the topic of the chapter as well as the main grammar points. You will hear the conversation once from the audio through the QR codes.

New Vocabulary and New Expressions

This section provides the definition of new vocabulary and expressions presented in the conversation.

Conversation Tips

"Conversation Tips" is provided with a more detailed explanation to assist learners in fully understanding the meaning of the phrase beyond just the grammar.

Pronunciation

This section highlights vocabulary from the conversation that is either representative of the pronunciation principles or particularly hard to pronounce. You will hear the words once from the audio via the QR code.

Additional Vocabulary

This section provides additional vocabulary related to the topic or useful for the exercises.

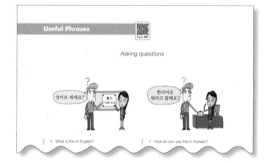

Useful Phrases

This section provides additional phrases related to the topic. Although these phrases may contain unfamiliar grammar, they are emphasized due to frequent use in everyday life. In order to assist learners, the phrases are presented with pictures as well.

Quiz Yourself!

This section has been divided into three parts: Grammar, Listening and Reading. Students may be able to quiz themselves after each chapter.

Contents

Introduction to Hangeul 13

Hangeul 1 17

Hangeul 2 25

Hangeul 3 35

Hangeul 4 45

Chapter 1   안녕하세요? 저는 폴이에요. Hello. I'm Paul. 63

Chapter 2   아니요, 회사원이에요. No, I am an office worker. 73

Chapter 3   이게 뭐예요? What is this? 83

Chapter 4   화장실이 어디에 있어요? Where is the bathroom? 93

Chapter 5   동생이 몇 명 있어요? How many younger siblings do you have? 103

Chapter 6   전화번호가 몇 번이에요? What is your phone number? 113

Chapter 7   생일이 며칠이에요? What day is your birthday? 123

Chapter 8   보통 아침 8시 30분에 회사에 가요.
I usually go to the office at 8:30 in the morning. 133

Chapter 9   집에 지하철로 가요. I go home by subway. 143

Chapter 10 전부 얼마예요? How much is it all together? 153

Chapter 11 어디에서 저녁 식사해요? Where do you have dinner? 163

Chapter 12 매주 일요일에 영화를 봐요. I see a movie every Sunday. 173

Chapter 13 머리가 아파요. I have a headache. 183

Chapter 14 지난주에 제주도에 여행 갔어요. Last week I traveled to Jeju Island. .. 193

Chapter 15 내일 한국 음식을 만들 거예요. I will make Korean food tomorrow. .. 203

Chapter 16 같이 영화 보러 갈 수 있어요? Should we go see a movie together? .. 213

Chapter 17 미안하지만, 다시 한번 말해 주세요.
I'm sorry but please say it again. 223

Chapter 18 저도 한국어를 배우고 싶어요. I also want to learn Korean. 233

Chapter 19 그다음에 오른쪽으로 가세요. After that please go to the right. 243

Chapter 20 성함이 어떻게 되세요? What is your name? 253

Appendix 263

Table of Contents

Chapter	Contents	
Introduction to Hangeul	Hangeul, the Korean writing system	
Hangeul 1	▪ The basic six vowels: ㅏ, ㅓ, ㅗ, ㅜ, ㅡ, ㅣ	▪ The basic five consonants: ㄱ, ㄴ, ㅁ, ㅅ, ㅇ
Hangeul 2	▪ Four combined vowels with [y]: ㅑ, ㅕ, ㅛ, ㅠ	▪ Five consonants: ㄷ, ㄹ, ㅂ, ㅈ, ㅎ
Hangeul 3	▪ Four vowels: ㅐ, ㅔ, ㅒ, ㅖ	▪ Four aspirated consonants: ㅋ, ㅌ, ㅍ, ㅊ
Hangeul 4	▪ Seven vowel combinations: ㅘ, ㅝ, ㅙ, ㅞ, ㅚ, ㅟ, ㅢ	▪ Five tensed consonants: ㄲ, ㄸ, ㅃ, ㅆ, ㅉ

Chapter	Topic	Title	Grammar	
1	Greetings	안녕하세요? 저는 폴이에요.	▪ -예요/이에요 "am/is/are" ▪ The topic marker 은/는	▪ The question words 뭐 "what" and 어느 "which" ▪ Countries and Nationalities
2	Jobs	아니요, 회사원이에요.	▪ 네 "yes" and 아니요 "no" ▪ Asking questions	▪ Leaving out the subject of a sentence ▪ Languages
3	Objects	이게 뭐예요?	▪ 이, 그, 저 "this, that, that" ▪ The subject marker 이/가	▪ The question words 무슨 "what kind of" and 누구 "who, whose" ▪ Possessives
4	Places	화장실이 어디에 있어요?	▪ 있어요 "there is(are)" and 없어요 "there is(are) not" ▪ The question word 어디 "where"	▪ The place marker 에 ▪ Location-based expressions
5	Relationships and possessions	동생이 몇 명 있어요?	▪ 있어요 "have" and 없어요 "don't have" ▪ Counting words	▪ Native Korean numbers ▪ The question word 몇 "how many"
6	Phone numbers	전화번호가 몇 번이에요?	▪ Sino-Korean numbers ▪ The question word 몇 번 "what number" ▪ How to read Sino-Korean numbers	▪ Reading phone numbers ▪ 이/가 아니에요 "is not ⋯ (noun)"
7	Birthdays	생일이 며칠이에요?	▪ Reading dates (year, month, day) ▪ 요일 Days of the week	▪ The question words 언제 "when" and 며칠 "what day" ▪ The time marker 에
8	Everyday life	보통 아침 8시 30분에 회사에 가요.	▪ Expressing time ▪ The marker for destination 에	▪ The question words 몇 시 "what time" and 몇 시에 "what time" ▪ The time markers ⋯부터 ⋯까지 "from ⋯ to ⋯"
9	Transportation	집에 지하철로 가요.	▪ Time duration ▪ The question words 어떻게 "how" and 얼마나 "how long/how much time"	▪ The markers ⋯에서 ⋯까지 "from ⋯ to ⋯" ▪ The marker (으)로: means of transportation
10	Buying things	전부 얼마예요?	▪ Reading prices ▪ (noun) 주세요 "Give me (noun) please"	▪ The question word 얼마 "how much" ▪ The marker 하고 "and" (used only with nouns)
11	A day's work	어디에서 저녁 식사해요?	▪ 하다 verbs "to do" ▪ Frequency	▪ The place marker 에서 ▪ The marker 하고 "with"
12	Hobbies	매주 일요일에 영화를 봐요.	▪ The informal polite form -아/어요 in the present tense ▪ Making suggestions "let's"	▪ The object marker 을/를 ▪ (noun)은/는 어때요? "how about (noun)?"
13	Health	머리가 아파요.	▪ The descriptive use of the adjectives -아/어요 in the present tense ▪ The marker 도 "also"	▪ Negating with 안
14	Travel	지난주에 제주도에 여행 갔어요.	▪ The informal polite form of the verbs and adjectives -았/었어요 in the past tense ▪ The superlative 제일 "the most"	▪ The word for time duration 동안 ▪ Comparison using 보다 더 "more than"
15	Plans	내일 한국 음식을 만들 거예요.	▪ The informal polite form of the verbs -(으)ㄹ 거예요 in the future tense	▪ Negating with 못 "cannot"
16	Appointments	같이 영화 보러 갈 수 있어요?	▪ -(으)ㄹ 수 있다/없다 "can/cannot" ▪ Expressing strong intent -(으)ㄹ게요 "I will"	▪ -(으)러 가다/오다 "to go/come in order to (verb)"
17	Favors	미안하지만, 다시 한번 말해 주세요.	▪ -아/어 주세요 "Please do (verb) for me."	▪ Confirming information -요?
18	Recommendations	저도 한국어를 배우고 싶어요.	▪ -고 싶다 "to want to (verb)" ▪ The grammar pattern for meaning attempting -아/어 보다 "to try to (verb)"	▪ Questions with -지 않아요? "isn't it?"
19	Taking taxis	그다음에 오른쪽으로 가세요.	▪ The grammar pattern for commands with -(으)세요 ▪ The formal polite form -(스)ㅂ니다	▪ Abbreviated questions
20	Making reservations	성함이 어떻게 되세요?	▪ Honorific language for the subject of a sentence	▪ Honorific language for the listener

Contents

- Ten final consonants: ㄱ, ㄴ, ㄹ, ㅁ, ㅂ, ㅇ, ㄷ, ㅅ, ㅈ, ㅎ
- Four final consonants: ㅋ, ㅌ, ㅍ, ㅊ
- Two final consonants: ㄲ, ㅆ
- Double final consonants: ㄵ, ㄶ, ㄼ, ㅄ, ㄺ, ㄻ

	Situation 1	Situation 2	A Word on Culture
	Asking someone's name	Asking someone's nationality	Don't say "you"!
	Guessing someone's job	Asking someone's job	Different language for different occasions
	Asking the name of something	Asking who owns something	Koreans like to say 우리
	Asking location	Asking for directions to someone's house over the phone	Seoul's sites
	Asking about possessions	Asking about someone's family relationships	Family titles
	Asking someone's phone number	Asking about and confirming someone's phone number	Counting age
	Inviting someone to a birthday party	Congratulating someone on his birthday	Korean birthday parties
	Talking about work	Talking about school	Greetings in Korean
	Asking how long something takes	Asking about means of transportation	Seoul's public transportation
	Ordering food	Buying train tickets	Unwritten rules about paying the bill
	Talking about daily tasks	Speaking about frequency	Communicating respect with one's hands
	Speaking about hobbies (Korean films)	Speaking about hobbies (Korean food)	The "Korean wave"
	Asking about a friend's health	Listening to someone's symptoms	A common response: 괜찮아요
	Asking about someone's trip	Talking about sightseeing	Interesting sights
	Making plans	Speaking about plans	Giving presents
	Suggesting some activity	Refusing someone's proposal	Modesty is a virtue?
	Confirming the location of an appointment over the phone	Asking a phone caller to wait	Speaking to someone for the first time
	Suggesting that someone learn Korean	Recommending food and a travel destination	A culture of affection
	Taking a taxi	Giving directions	When do I need to use formal language?
	Making a restaurant reservation over the phone	Making hotel reservations over the phone	Food on special occasions

Introduction to Hangeul

Hangeul was created by King Sejong with a group of scholars in 1443 and promulgated in 1446. Hangeul is still used today as the Korean writing system. Until that time, spoken Korean was rendered into writing using classical Chinese characters, which could only be mastered after years of intense study (and therefore only used by the literati). Hangeul is a distinctive writing system for the following reason. Although it is an alphabet, it is written in syllables rather than one letter following another. The shapes of the vowels and consonants symbolize nature and the physical processes used to pronounce each sound. Perhaps its strongest virtue is that it is easy enough for anyone to learn. Not convinced yet? As the Koreans say, 시작이 반이다(starting is half the bottle). So let's begin.

⬤ Origin of vowels in Hangeul

Vowels in Hangeul symbolize natural phenomena. Vowels are built from the following elements: '·' (representing heaven/sky), '—' (representing land/earth), and '|' (representing a person). So, for instance, '|' with '·' to the right combine to make '|'. At present there are twenty-one vowels in modern Korean.

⬤ Origin of consonants in Hangeul

'ㄱ, ㄴ, ㅁ, ㅅ, ㅇ' are the basic consonants in Korean, and each consonant's shape depicts the position of the tongue, lips, or throat, when uttering the sound.

For instance, the consonant 'ㄴ' comes from the tongue touching the roof of the mouth, and the shape of 'ㄴ' is meant to depict the tongue in that position. At present there are nineteen consonants in Korean.

How does one construct syllables in Hangeul?

In Hangeul, each syllable must have a vowel. So it is helpful to think of each syllable as centered around the vowel, where the vowel may be combined with one or two consonant sounds.

Let's examine the methods by which the syllables are composed, where V stands for a vowel, and C for a consonant.

1   **When a vowel stands by itself (no consonants):**
    There are two types of vowels: vertical vowels (vowels which are written on the right) and horizontal vowels (vowels which are written below).

    V   아   우

2   **When a consonant and a vowel occur together, with the consonant sound occurring first:**

    C V   나   누

3   **When a vowel and a consonant occur together, with the consonant sound written last:**
    The final consonant is called "batchim" to distinguish it from the initial consonant.

    V
    C   안   운

4   **When a vowel occurs between consonants:**
    The consonants are combined before a vowel and after a vowel. The important thing is that one or two consonants that follow a vowel can be spelled together, but the pronunciation is uttered as one.

    C V
    C   난   눈   밖   닭

    * Please note that although most of the time there is only one final consonant, occasionally there will be two.

How does one write the syllables?

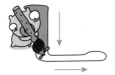

When writing Hangeul, you should follow two rules. First, write from top to bottom, and second, from left to right.

How are English words pronounced in Korean?

One general rule of pronouncing Korean is that each consonant needs a vowel to be pronounced and made into a syllable. Without the vowel's help, a consonant cannot stand alone as an independent syllable.

Writing/pronouncing English words in Korean is no exception to the rule. For example, 'love', which has one vowel 'o' for the consonant 'l' and 'e' for 'v', is pronounced 'lo-ve' (러-브) as two syllables.

But a word such as 'skirt', which has only one vowel 'i' for consonants 's,k,r, t', must be broken into multiple syllables in Korean: 's-kir-t' (스-커-트) as three syllables.

In the next four chapters we'll examine more concretely how to put consonants and vowels together.

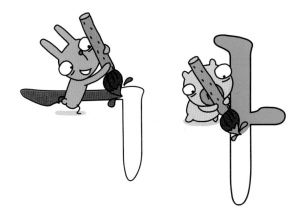

Hangeul 1

- The basic six vowels ㅏ ㅓ ㅗ ㅜ ㅡ ㅣ
- The basic five consonants ㄱ ㄴ ㅁ ㅅ ㅇ

The following are the basic six vowels.

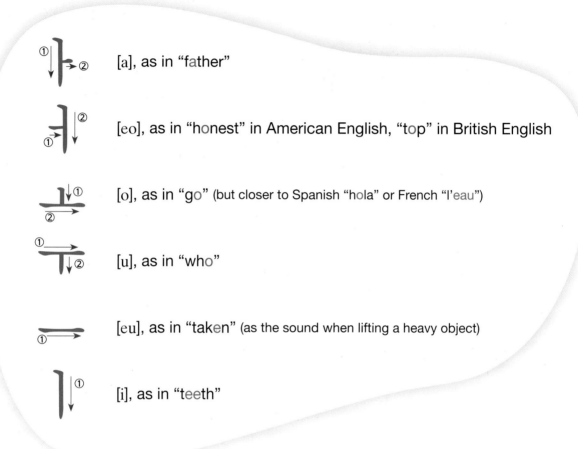

[a], as in "father"

[eo], as in "honest" in American English, "top" in British English

[o], as in "go" (but closer to Spanish "hola" or French "l'eau")

[u], as in "who"

[eu], as in "taken" (as the sound when lifting a heavy object)

[i], as in "teeth"

● Silent 'ㅇ'

In Hangeul, one can form a syllable with one vowel without using any consonant sound before the vowel. To write a syllable, you can put a silent 'ㅇ' that acts like a consonant in front of the vowel to replace the missing consonant. For a similar connection in English, think of the letter 'ㅇ' in Hangeul as the **silent** [y] in the alphabet as it does not produce any sound in the beginning of the word 'year'.

● Vertical vowels and horizontal vowels

Vowels which are formed from the basic symbol 'ㅣ', namely, 'ㅏ, ㅓ, ㅣ' are vertical vowels, and those formed from 'ㅡ', in other words, 'ㅗ, ㅜ, ㅡ' are horizontal vowels. When combined with consonants or the silent 'ㅇ', vertical vowels are placed to the right of the initial consonant (or 'ㅇ'), and horizontal vowels are placed below.

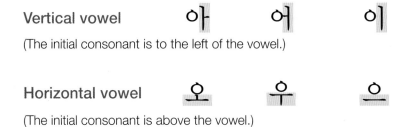

Vertical vowel   아   어   이
(The initial consonant is to the left of the vowel.)

Horizontal vowel   오   우   으
(The initial consonant is above the vowel.)

The pronunciation of vowels is differentiated by the amount one opens one's mouth and the position of the tongue. Please look at the pictures and follow along.

Track **001**

open   아   어

round   오   우

flat   으   이

	이	이	이
teeth			

	이	이	이
two			

	오	오	오
five			

	아이	아이	아이
child			

	오이	오이	오이
cucumber			

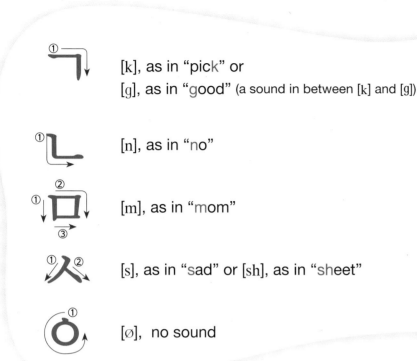

[k], as in "pick" or
[g], as in "good" (a sound in between [k] and [g])

[n], as in "no"

[m], as in "mom"

[s], as in "sad" or [sh], as in "sheet"

[ø], no sound

Making consonants

As mentioned above, the shapes of basic consonants mimic the organs of their vocalization (tongue, lips, throat) as the sounds are being pronounced.

The shape of 'ㄱ'([k] or [g]) mimics the tongue in this position.

The shape of 'ㄴ'[n] mimics the tongue in this position.

The shape of 'ㅁ'[m] mimics an open mouth.

The shape of 'ㅅ'([s] or [sh]) mimics the air flow in that position.

The shape of 'ㅇ' mimics the shape of an open throat.

When combining consonants and vowels, replace the silent 'ㅇ' with a consonant.

Track 003

When 'ㄱ' is combined with a horizontal vowel, the shape is almost a right angle. (Ex. 고, 구, 그)
When 'ㄱ' is combined with a vertical vowel, the bottom part curves a bit. (Ex. 가, 거, 기)

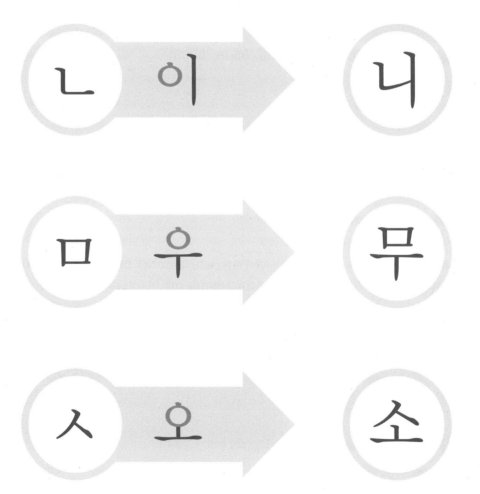

When 'ㅅ' is combined with the vowel 'ㅣ, ㅑ, ㅕ, ㅛ, ㅠ', 'ㅅ' is pronounced as [sh].

나무
나무

tree

고기
고기

meat

소
소

cow

나이
나이

age

어머니
어머니

mother

가수
가수

singer

▸ Listen and mark O if correct or X if incorrect. (1~3)

1
어
( )

2
그
( )

3
노
( )

Track 005

▸ Listen and choose the correct answer. (4~7)

4 ⓐ 아 ⓑ 어 ⓒ 오 ⓓ 우

5 ⓐ 나 ⓑ 너 ⓒ 노 ⓓ 누

6 ⓐ 모 ⓑ 머 ⓒ 므 ⓓ 미

7 ⓐ 소 ⓑ 서 ⓒ 스 ⓓ 시

Track 006

▸ Listen and choose the correct answer. (8~10)

8 ⓐ 머리 ⓑ 모리

9 ⓐ 거기 ⓑ 고기

10 ⓐ 나무 ⓑ 너무

Track 007

▸ Listen and complete the word. (11~14)

11
□ 이

12
□

13
□ 수

14
나 □

Answers p.275

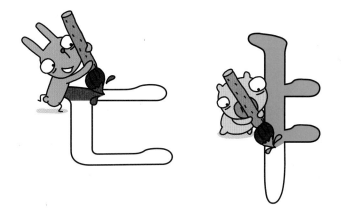

Hangeul 2

- Four combined vowels with [y] ㅑ ㅕ ㅛ ㅠ
- Five consonants ㄷ ㄹ ㅂ ㅈ ㅎ
- Ten final consonants ㄱ ㄴ ㄹ ㅁ ㅂ ㅇ ㄷ ㅅ ㅈ ㅎ

The basic vowels 'ㅏ, ㅓ, ㅗ, ㅜ' are combined with [y] to form the vowels 'ㅑ, ㅕ, ㅛ, ㅠ'. The mouth positions are the same.

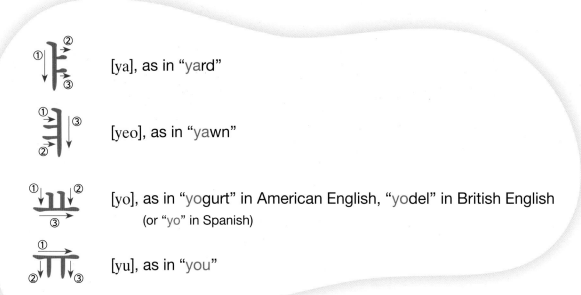

[ya], as in "yard"

[yeo], as in "yawn"

[yo], as in "yogurt" in American English, "yodel" in British English (or "yo" in Spanish)

[yu], as in "you"

Track **009**

우유
우유

milk

여기
여기

here

야구
야구

baseball

아니요
아니요

no

여우
여우

fox

가요
가요

go

Five consonants

The next five consonants are similar to the basic consonants, but with additional strokes. 'ㄷ' and 'ㄹ' are derived from 'ㄴ', 'ㅂ' is derived from 'ㅁ', 'ㅈ' is derived from 'ㅅ', and 'ㅎ' is derived from 'ㅇ'.

ㄷ   [t], as in "battle"
       [d], as in "deep"

ㄹ   [ℓ], as in "lollipop"
       [r], as in "x-ray"
       (as in the Spanish tapped "r" in "para")

ㅂ   [p], as in "pop"
       [b], as in "baby"

ㅈ   [j], as in "juice"

ㅎ   [h], as in "house"

Track 011

ㄷ 오	도
ㄹ 우	루
ㅂ 아	바
ㅈ 이	지
ㅎ 어	허

머리

머리

head

구두

구두

dress shoes

지도

지도

map

바다

바다

sea

아버지

아버지

father

하나

하나

one

A consonant which occurs below the vowel is called a final consonant ("batchim") and is pronounced after the vowel. In most cases, the pronunciation of the final consonant is the same as when it is pronounced as an initial sound. 'ㅇ' is soundless as an initial consonant but is pronounced as [ng] when it occurs as a final consonant. And 'ㄷ, ㅅ, ㅈ, ㅎ' are all pronounced as [t] when they occur as final consonants.

ㄱ   [k], as in "cook"

ㄴ   [n], as in "noon"

ㄹ   [ℓ], as in "hello"

ㅁ   [m], as in "hum"

ㅂ   [p], as in "chop"

ㅇ   [ng], as in "ring"

ㄷ = ㅅ = ㅈ = ㅎ   [t], as in "get"

Remember that there are only seven possible pronuncations for final consonants.

Track 013

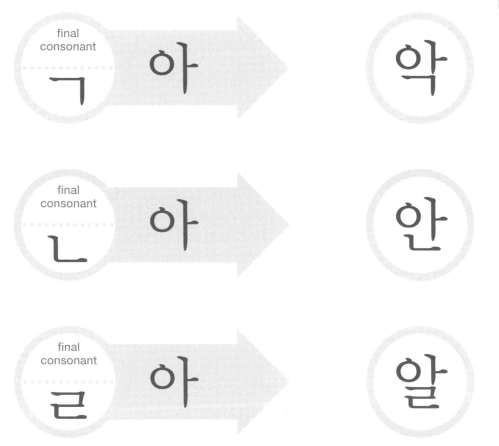

When '근' occurs between two vowel sounds (Ex. 머리), it is pronounced close to [r].
When '근' occurs as a final consonant (Ex. 알), it is pronounced more like [ℓ].

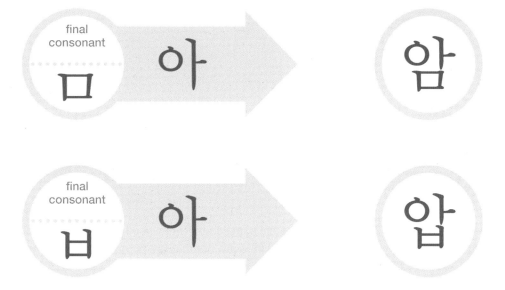

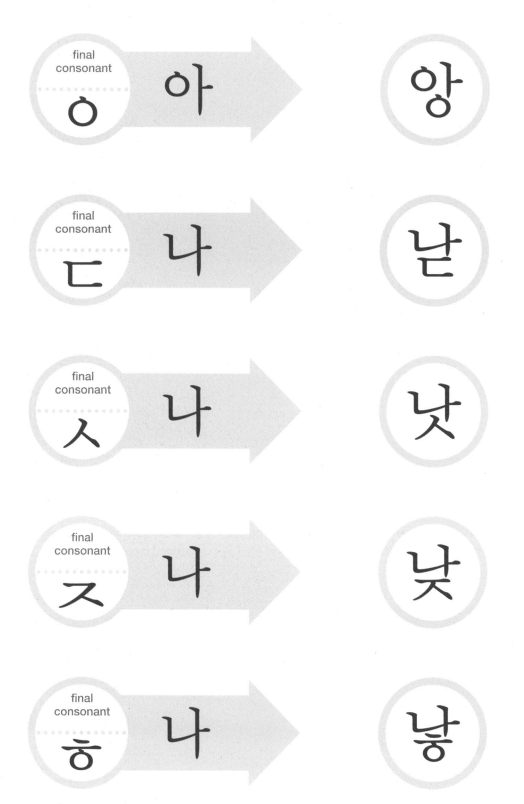

Remember that '은, ᄉ, ᄌ, ᄒ' produce the same sound when used as final consonants. In other words, 낟, 낫, 낮, 낳 are spelled differently, but they are pronounced the same.

물

물

water

집

집

house

미국

미국

U.S.A.

남자

남자

man

안경

안경

eyeglasses

옷

옷

clothes

▸ Listen and choose the correct answer. (1~8)

Track 015

1	ⓐ 요가	ⓑ 여가	
2	ⓐ 유리	ⓑ 여리	
3	ⓐ 논	ⓑ 돈	
4	ⓐ 몸	ⓑ 봄	
5	ⓐ 거리	ⓑ 허리	
6	ⓐ 수소	ⓑ 주소	
7	ⓐ 짐	ⓑ 집	
8	ⓐ 사람	ⓑ 사랑	

▸ Listen and choose the correct answer to complete the word. (9~14)

Track 016

9	☐다	ⓐ 마	ⓑ 바	ⓒ 나	ⓓ 다
10	☐구	ⓐ 야	ⓑ 여	ⓒ 요	ⓓ 유
11	구☐	ⓐ 더	ⓑ 도	ⓒ 두	ⓓ 드
12	아☐지	ⓐ 바	ⓑ 버	ⓒ 보	ⓓ 부
13	가☐	ⓐ 반	ⓑ 밤	ⓒ 박	ⓓ 방
14	☐자	ⓐ 난	ⓑ 남	ⓒ 낙	ⓓ 낭

▸ Listen and complete the word. (15~20)

Track 017

Answers p.275

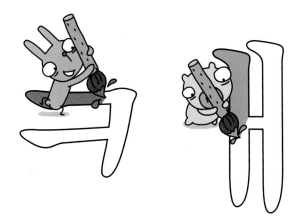

Hangeul 3

- Four vowels 　ㅒㅖㅖㅋ
- Four aspirated consonants　ㅋ ㅌ ㅍ ㅊ
- Four final consonants　ㅋ ㅌ ㅍ ㅊ

The following vowels have similar sounds.

The vowel 'ㅐ' is a combination of two simple vowels, 'ㅏ + ㅣ = ㅐ'. Likewise 'ㅔ' is a combination of 'ㅓ' and 'ㅣ'. Strictly speaking, the vowels 'ㅐ' and 'ㅔ' are different sounds, but they are pronounced similarly. The vowels 'ㅒ' and 'ㅖ' are combined of 'ㅐ' and 'ㅔ' with [y]. They too are different sounds, but are pronounced similarly in real life.

Track 018

ㅏ + ㅣ   애

ㅓ + ㅣ   에

애 ▶ 얘

에 ▶ 예

The pronunciation of the above vowels is hard to distinguish in everyday speech. For practical purposes, you can consider the pronunciations the same, "and" and "end" (ㅐ = ㅔ), or "yet" (ㅒ = ㅖ). You can consider the pronunciations the same as '애 =에' and '얘=예'.

Track 019

노래

노래

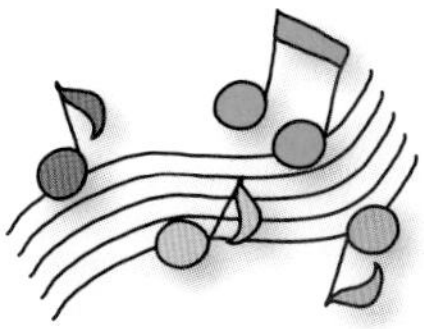

song

아내

아내

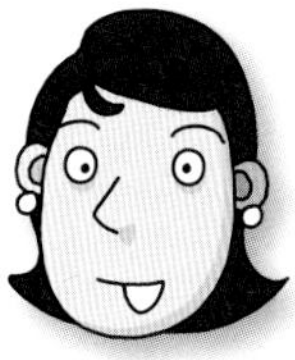

wife

가게

가게

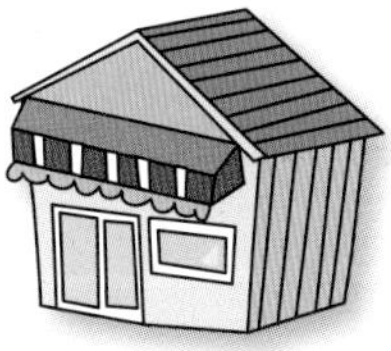

store

어제

어제

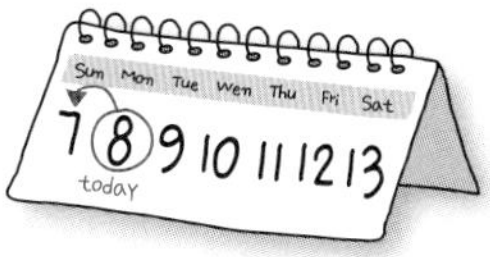

yesterday

시계

시계

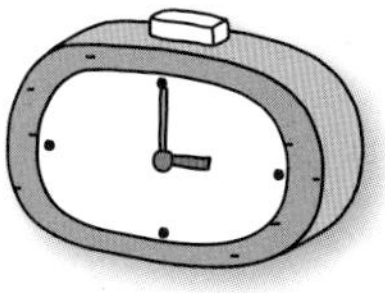

clock

얘기

얘기

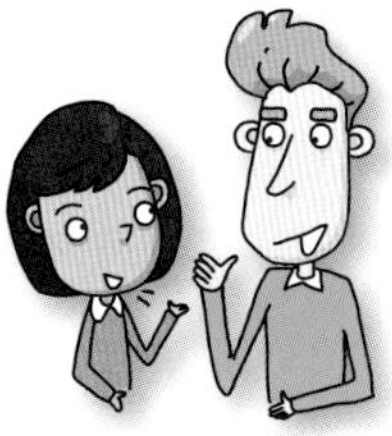

talk

The consonants '∃, ㅌ, ㅍ, ㅊ' are derived from the following consonants 'ㄱ, ㄷ, ㅂ, ㅈ', but with a stronger release of air. '∃' is derived from 'ㄱ', 'ㅌ' is derived from 'ㄷ', 'ㅍ' is derived from 'ㅂ', and 'ㅊ' is derived from 'ㅈ'.

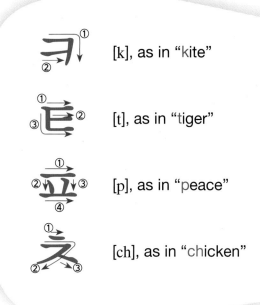

[k], as in "kite"

[t], as in "tiger"

[p], as in "peace"

[ch], as in "chicken"

Track 020

When '∃' is combined with a horizontal vowel, the shape is almost a right angle. (Ex. 코, 쿠, 크)
When '∃' is combined with a vertical vowel, the bottom part curves a bit. (Ex. 카, 커, 키)

ㅌ + ㅗ → 토

ㅍ + ㅓ → 퍼

ㅊ + ㅜ → 추

Track 021

! Be careful

Let's learn how to pronounce the following Hangeul.

가 카　　도 토

버 퍼　　즈 츠

지하철
지하철

subway

표
표

ticket

토요일
토요일

Saturday

코
코

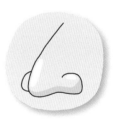

nose

커피
커피

coffee

주차장
주차장

parking lot

Four final consonants

When they occur as final consonants, these consonants are read as follows.

ㅋ = ㄱ [k]

ㅍ = ㅂ [p]

ㅌ = ㄷ [t]

ㅊ = ㅈ = ㄷ [t]

Track 023

final consonant ㅋ + 어 → 엌

final consonant ㅍ + 아 → 앞

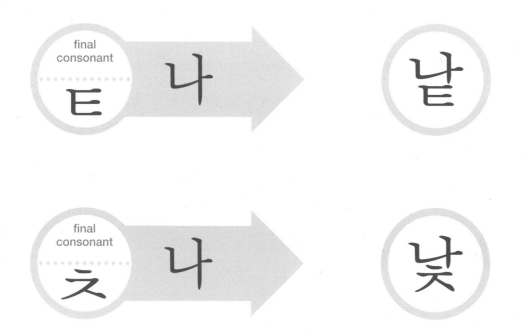

Notice that 낟, 낱, 낫, 낫, 낮, 낳 are spelled differently, but they are pronounced the same.

Track 024

! Be careful

Let's learn how to pronounce the following Hangeul.

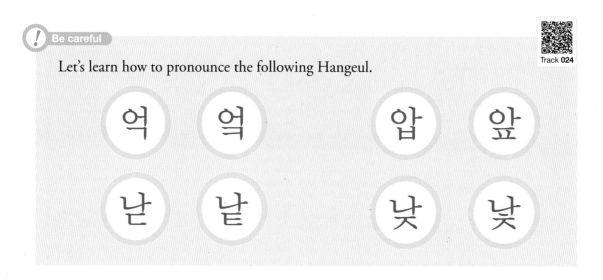

국

국

soup

부엌

부엌

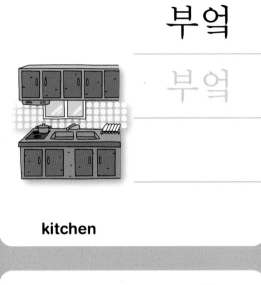

kitchen

빗

빗

comb

빛

빛

ray of light

입

입

mouth

잎

잎

leaf

Quiz Yourself!

▶ Listen and choose the correct answer. (1~6)

1 ⓐ 보도　　ⓑ 포도　　2 ⓐ 누리　　ⓑ 두리

3 ⓐ 만금　　ⓑ 만큼　　4 ⓐ 기자　　ⓑ 기차

5 ⓐ 여리　　ⓑ 예리　　6 ⓐ 애기　　ⓑ 애기

▶ Listen and choose the correct answer to complete the word. (7~10)

7 김☐　　ⓐ 시　　ⓑ 지　　ⓒ 치　　ⓓ 히

8 ☐도　　ⓐ 모　　ⓑ 보　　ⓒ 포　　ⓓ 호

9 ☐기　　ⓐ 그　　ⓑ 크　　ⓒ 구　　ⓓ 쿠

10 ☐수　　ⓐ 드　　ⓑ 트　　ⓒ 두　　ⓓ 투

▶ Choose the pronunciation that is different from the rest. Cross check the answer by listening to the audio. (11~13)

11 ⓐ 빗　　ⓑ 빕　　ⓒ 빗　　ⓓ 빛

12 ⓐ 믹　　ⓑ 믿　　ⓒ 밑　　ⓓ 및

13 ⓐ 순　　ⓑ 숫　　ⓒ 숯　　ⓓ 숲

▶ Listen and complete the word. (14~19)

14 | ㅖ | ㅡ |

15 | ㅖ | ㅏ |

16 | ㅏ | ㅖ | ㅏ |

17 | ㅓ | ㅠ | ㅓ |

18 | ㅍ |

19 | ㅊ |

Answers p.275

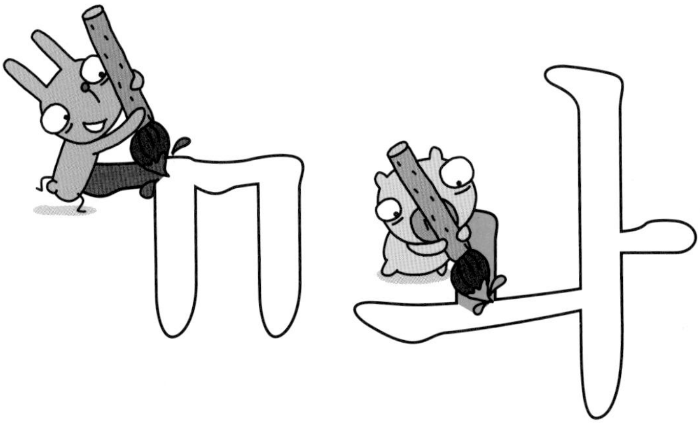

Hangeul 4

- Seven vowel combinations ㅘ ㅝ ㅙ ㅞ ㅚ ㅟ ㅢ
- Five tensed consonants ㄲ ㄸ ㅃ ㅆ ㅉ
- Two final consonants ㄲ ㅆ
- Double final consonants ㄵ ㄶ ㄼ ㅄ ㄺ ㄻ

Seven vowel combinations

The following is an introduction to seven vowels which are combinations of two vowels.

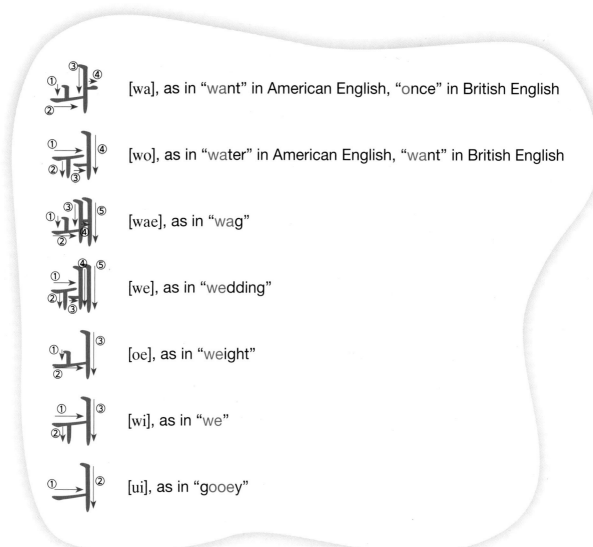

[wa], as in "want" in American English, "once" in British English

[wo], as in "water" in American English, "want" in British English

[wae], as in "wag"

[we], as in "wedding"

[oe], as in "weight"

[wi], as in "we"

[ui], as in "gooey"

In English, the sound of the vowel 'ㅢ' [ui] as in "gooey" is pronounced as two syllables. Try to say these two syllables quickly, as one syllable, and you will be able to make the sound of the Korean vowel 'ㅢ'.

Track 030

ㅗ + ㅏ　와

ㅜ + ㅓ　워

ㅗ + ㅐ　왜

ㅜ + ㅔ　웨

ㅗ + ㅣ　외

ㅜ + ㅣ　위

ㅡ + ㅣ　의

사과
사과

apple

돼지
돼지

pig

병원
병원

hospital

외국인
외국인

foreigner

귀
귀

ear

의자
의자

chair

The following consonants are derived from the basic consonants, but these consonants are pronounced by tensing your throat (as in the case when you are angry). 'ㄲ' is derived from 'ㄱ', 'ㅃ' is derived from 'ㅂ', 'ㄸ' is derived from 'ㄷ', 'ㅆ' is derived from 'ㅅ', and 'ㅉ' is derived from 'ㅈ'.

ㄲ   [kk], as in "gotcha!"

ㄸ   [tt], as in "Duh!"

ㅃ   [pp], as in "Bad!"

ㅆ   [ss], as in "sang!" (with a tense throat)

ㅉ   [jj], as in "gotcha!"

Track 032

ㄲ + 아 → 까

ㄸ + 오 → 또

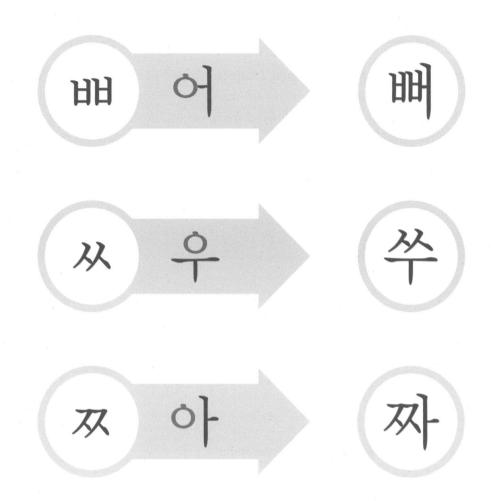

Track 033

!

Let's learn how to pronounce the following Hangeul.

| 가 | 카 | 까 | | 도 | 토 | 또 |

| 버 | 퍼 | 뻐 | | 수 | | 쑤 |

| 자 | 차 | 짜 |

빵
빵

bread

어깨
어깨

shoulders

땀
땀

sweat

토끼
토끼

rabbit

비싸요
비싸요

expensive

짜요
짜요

salty

Two final consonants

When '11' and 'ㅆ' occur as final consonants, they are pronounced as follows.

$$\text{ㄲ = ㅋ = ㄱ} \quad \text{[k]}$$

$$\text{ㅆ = ㅅ = ㄷ} \quad \text{[t]}$$

final consonant
ㄲ 바 → 밖

Track 035

final consonant
ㅆ 가 → 갔

Double final consonants

Occasionally two consonants appear below the vowel; this is called a double final consonant. Sometimes only the first consonant is pronounced and sometimes only the second one is pronounced.

In words with these double final consonants 'ㄵ, ㄶ, ㄼ, ㅄ', only the first final consonant is pronounced.

앉다   않다   여덟   값

In words with these double final consonants 'ㄺ, ㄻ', only the second final consonant is pronounced.

닭   삶

밖

밖

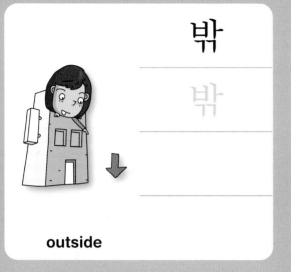

outside

갔다

갔다

Yesterday

went

닭

닭

chicken

여덟

여덟

eight

값

값

BOOK

₩9,500

price

앉다

앉다

sit

▶ Listen and choose the correct answer. (1~5)

Track 037

1 ⓐ 자요   ⓑ 차요   ⓒ 짜요

2 ⓐ 달   ⓑ 탈   ⓒ 딸

3 ⓐ 방   ⓑ 팡   ⓒ 빵

4 ⓐ 외   ⓑ 위   ⓒ 와

5 ⓐ 의자   ⓑ 위자   ⓒ 외자

▶ Listen and choose the correct answer to complete the word. (6~10)

Track 038

6 아☐   ⓐ 마   ⓑ 바   ⓒ 파   ⓓ 빠

7 ☐요   ⓐ 사   ⓑ 자   ⓒ 싸   ⓓ 짜

8 더☐요   ⓐ 오   ⓑ 어   ⓒ 우   ⓓ 워

9 ☐자   ⓐ 궈   ⓑ 과   ⓒ 궤   ⓓ 괘

10 ☐사   ⓐ 호   ⓑ 회   ⓒ 후   ⓓ 휘

▶ Listen and complete the word. (11~16)

Track 039

11 | ㅇ | ㅈ |

12 | ㅅ | ㄱ |

13 | ㅗ | ㅏ |

14 | ㅏ | ㅣ |

15 | ㅈ | ㅊ |

16 | ㅁ | ㄹ |

Answers p.275

All twenty-one vowels

single	combination with [y]	single	combination with [y]
ㅏ	ㅑ	ㅓ	ㅕ
[a] father	[ya] yard	[eo] honest, top	[yeo] yawn
ㅗ	ㅛ	ㅜ	ㅠ
[o] go	[yo] yogurt, yodel	[u] who	[yu] you
―		ㅣ	
[eu] taken		[i] teeth	
ㅐ	ㅒ	ㅔ	ㅖ
[ae] at, any	[yae] yak	[e] end, every	[ye] yes

[w] vowels		the other vowel
ㅘ	ㅝ	
[wa] want, once	[wo] water	
ㅙ	ㅞ	ㅢ
[wae] wag	[we] wedding	[ui] gooey
ㅚ	ㅟ	
[oe] weight	[wi] we	

All nineteen consonants

★ Depending on the strength of the air

- Basic consonants (Pronounce by not using much air)
- Aspirated consonants (Pronounce by using a lot of air)
- Tensed consonants (Pronounce stronger with a tight throat, not using much air)

The method of pronunciation	The position of pronunciation	Bilabial sound (Pronounce using the lips)		Alveolar sound (Pronounce by touching the end of the tongue behind the upper teeth)	
Plosive (Pronounce by puffing strong air)	Basic consonants	ㅂ	[b] baby [p] pop	ㄷ	[d] deep [t] battle
	Aspirated consonants	ㅍ	[p] peace	ㅌ	[t] tiger
	Tensed consonants	ㅃ	[pp] Bad!	ㄸ	[tt] Duh! (Strong pronunciation)
Fricative (Pronounce with friction via a narrowed articulator organ)	Basic consonants			ㅅ	[s] sad [sh] sheet (In front of the vowels ㅣ, ㅑ, ㅕ, ㅛ and ㅠ)
	Tensed consonants			ㅆ	[ss] sang!
Affricate (Pronounce by puffing air with friction)	Basic consonants				
	Aspirated consonants				
	Tensed consonants				
Nasal (Pronounce by using the nose)		ㅁ	[m] mom	ㄴ	[n] no, now
Liquid [ɾ] (Pronounce by touching the end of the tongue behind the upper teeth) [ℓ] (Pronounce by placing the tip of the tongue on the upper gum and let the air flow from side to side)				ㄹ	[ɾ] X-ray [ℓ] lollipop

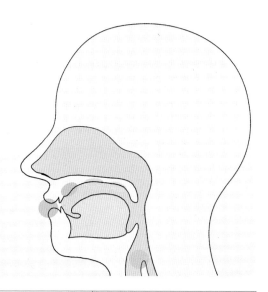

Palatal sound (Pronounce by touching the tongue along the front palate)		Velar sound (Pronounce by touching the tongue on the back of the palate)		Glottal sound (Pronounce with the larynx)	
		ㄱ	[g] good [k] pick		
		ㅋ	[k] kite		
		ㄲ	[kk] gotcha!		
				ㅎ	[h] house
ㅈ	[j] juice				
ㅊ	[ch] chicken				
ㅉ	[jj] gotcha!				
		ㅇ	[ng] ring (Pronounce only in the final consonants)		

Final consonants only come in seven sounds

Although any consonant can be written as a final consonant, some of the consonants are not pronounced as they are in the initial position. Thus, all those written consonants boil down to only seven possible sounds in the final consonant position.

[p]	ㅂ	입	ㅍ	잎		
[m]	ㅁ	님				
[n]	ㄴ	산				
[ℓ]	ㄹ	물				
[k]	ㄱ	국	ㅋ	부엌	ㄲ	밖
[ng]	ㅇ	강				
[t]	ㄷ	듣다	ㅌ	끝		
	ㅅ	빗			ㅆ	갔다
	ㅈ	빚	ㅊ	빛		
	ㅎ	낳다				

Comparison of Korean and English

Let's take a minute to examine some of the main differences between Korean and English.

1. **The verb comes last.**

   마크(Mark) 음식(food) 먹어요(eats).

   Unlike in English, in Korean, the verb always appears last in the sentence. So the order of the sentence is usually: subject, object, verb.

2. **Korean has markers.**

   subject marker   object marker

   마크(Mark)가 음식(food)을 먹어요(eats).
   who   what

   Although the verb is always last, the order of the other parts of the sentence is not very strict in Korean. That is because, unlike English, Korean has markers which define what role different words play in a sentence (subject, object, etc.).

3. **The order of questions and answers are the same.**

   Question   마크(Mark)가 뭐(what) 먹어요(eats)?
   Answer   마크(Mark)가 음식(food)을 먹어요(eats).

   In Korean, the sentence structure of the question and its answer are the same. However, questions end with a rising tone and declarative sentences end with a slightly falling tone.

Hangeul pronunciation table

Consonants / Vowels	ㄱ	ㄴ	ㄷ	ㄹ	ㅁ	ㅂ
ㅏ	가	나	다	라	마	바
ㅑ	갸	냐	댜	랴	먀	뱌
ㅓ	거	너	더	러	머	버
ㅕ	겨	녀	뎌	려	며	벼
ㅗ	고	노	도	로	모	보
ㅛ	교	뇨	됴	료	묘	뵤
ㅜ	구	누	두	루	무	부
ㅠ	규	뉴	듀	류	뮤	뷰
ㅡ	그	느	드	르	므	브
ㅣ	기	니	디	리	미	비

ㅅ	ㅇ	ㅈ	ㅊ	ㅋ	ㅌ	ㅍ	ㅎ
사	아	자	차	카	타	파	하
샤	야	쟈	챠	캬	탸	퍄	햐
서	어	저	처	커	터	퍼	허
셔	여	져	쳐	켜	텨	펴	혀
소	오	조	초	코	토	포	호
쇼	요	죠	쵸	쿄	툐	표	효
수	우	주	추	쿠	투	푸	후
슈	유	쥬	츄	큐	튜	퓨	휴
스	으	즈	츠	크	트	프	흐
시	이	지	치	키	티	피	히

Meet the Main Characters!

제인 **Jane**
Canadian
English teacher

지나 **Jina**
Korean
Graduate student
Paul's friend

폴 **Paul**
Australian
University student

유진 **Yujin**
Korean
University student
James' student

진수 **Jinsu**
Korean
Office worker
Mark's friend

메이 **Mei**
Chinese
University
exchange student

마크 **Mark**
American
Office worker

제임스 **James**
English
English teacher

리에 **Rie**
Japanese
Japanese teacher
Jinsu's friend

Start to learn
Korean with us!

Chapter 1 　안녕하세요? 저는 폴이에요.

- -예요/이에요 "am/is/are"
- The question words 뭐 "what" and 어느 "which"
- The topic marker 은/는
- Countries and Nationalities

● **-예요/이에요** "am, is, are"

Appendix p.267

Think of this pattern as an equal sign; it helps describe some equivalence between two things (such as "I am Paul." or "She is a doctor.").

ending in a vowel	ending in a consonant
제임스예요. I am James.	폴이에요. I am Paul.

● **The question word 뭐** "what"

Use 뭐 like the English word "what" when asking questions.

A	이름이 뭐예요?		What is your name?
B	마크예요.		I am Mark.

 Be careful

뭐 is used together with -예요 to ask questions. 뭐예요 goes at the end of the sentence.

이름이 뭐예요? (O)
뭐 이름이에요? (x)

? I wonder...

While people use 뭐 in colloquial conversations, 무엇 is used in formal writing.

이름이 뭐예요?　　What is your name? [colloquial]
이름이 무엇입니까? What is your name? [formal]

The topic marker 은/는

The topic marker, as its name implies, designates the topic of a sentence. Not every sentence has to have a topic marker, however. Rather, the topic marker appears when one wants to stress a new topic. Think of how, when making introductions, you might use your hands to indicate the people to whom you're referring. When making introductions in Korean, the topic marker functions as this gesture, emphasizing each person in turn.

ending in a vowel	ending in a consonant
저는 폴이에요. I am Paul. (Introducing yourself.)	선생님은 한국 사람이에요. The teacher is Korean. (Indicating to someone that you're now speaking about the teacher.)

Countries and Nationalities

Describe someone's nationality by saying the country name and then the word 사람.

한국 Korea — 한국 사람 Korean

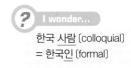

? I wonder...

한국 사람 [colloquial]
= 한국인 [formal]

The question word 어느 "which"

The question word 어느 followed by a noun allows you to ask someone to specify "which" among a category or group of objects.

A 어느 나라 사람이에요?   Which country are you from?

B 저는 호주 사람이에요.   I am Australian.

Track 041

Ann	Hello.
Satoru	Hello.
Ann	What's your name?
Satoru	I am Satoru. What is your name?
Ann	I am Ann. Nice to meet you.
Satoru	Nice to meet you.

앤	안녕하세요?
사토루	안녕하세요?
앤	이름이 뭐예요?
사토루	저는 사토루예요. 이름이 뭐예요?
앤	저는 앤이에요. 반갑습니다.
사토루	반갑습니다.

New Vocabulary

이름 name
뭐 what
저는 I

New Expressions

안녕하세요? Hello.
이름이 뭐예요?
What is your name?
반갑습니다. Nice to meet you.

Conversation Tips

★ 안녕하세요? "Hello."

Although this phrase is a greeting, you should pronounce it like a question, with your tone rising at the end. If you are meeting someone for the first time, bow your head a bit as you make your greeting.

Track 042

Mark	Hello. I am Mark.
Yujin	Hello. I am Yujin.
Mark	Yujin, which country are you from?
Yujin	I am Korean. Mark, which country are you from?
Mark	I am American.
	(The conversation continues for some time.)
Yujin	See you later.
Mark	See you later.

마크   안녕하세요? 저는 마크예요.

유진   안녕하세요? 저는 유진이에요.

마크   유진 씨, 어느 나라 사람이에요?

유진   저는 한국 사람이에요.

       마크 씨, 어느 나라 사람이에요?

마크   저는 미국 사람이에요.

(The conversation continues for some time.)

유진   다음에 또 봐요.

마크   다음에 또 봐요.

New Vocabulary

씨 Mr., Miss., Mrs.
어느 which
나라 country
사람 person
한국 Korea
한국 사람 Korean
미국 U.S.A.
미국 사람 American
다음에 next time
또 again
봐요 (I) see

New Expressions

어느 나라 사람이에요?
Which country are you from?

다음에 또 봐요. See you later.

Conversation Tips

★ **Use people's names rather than the pronoun "you"**

In Korean, it's not polite to use the pronoun "you" to someone you have just met. Instead, use the person's full name or given name followed by 씨 to indicate respect. But don't use 씨 when referring to yourself!

● 사람이에요 [사라미에요]

When a noun ends in a final consonant and is followed by a vowel, the final consonant is pronounced as if it is the initial consonant of the next syllable. But when the final consonant is 'ㅇ', pronounced as [ng] (such as 가방), the word is pronounced as written.

(1) 폴이에요 [포리에요]

(2) 선생님이에요 [선생니미에요]

(3) 가방이에요 [가방이에요]

Additional Vocabulary

Track **044**

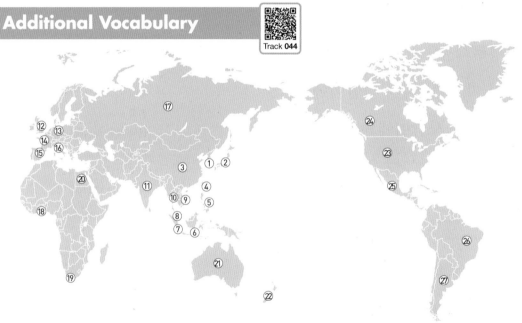

아시아	Asia	유럽	Europe	오세아니아	Oceania
1 한국	Korea	12 영국	Great Britain	21 호주	Australia
2 일본	Japan	13 독일	Germany	22 뉴질랜드	New Zealand
3 중국	China	14 프랑스	France		
4 대만	Taiwan	15 스페인	Spain	아메리카	America
5 필리핀	Philippines	16 이탈리아	Italy	23 미국	U.S.A.
6 인도네시아	Indonesia	17 러시아	Russia	24 캐나다	Canada
7 싱가포르	Singapore			25 멕시코	Mexico
8 말레이시아	Malaysia	아프리카	Africa	26 브라질	Brazil
9 베트남	Vietnam	18 가나	Ghana	27 아르헨티나	Argentina
10 태국	Thailand	19 남아프리카 공화국	South Africa		
11 인도	India	20 이집트	Egypt		

Hello and Goodbye

A   Hello.

B   Hello.

When meeting someone for the first time, bow your head to indicate respect.

A   Goodbye.

B   Goodbye.

When both are leaving.

A   Goodbye.

B   Goodbye.

When a person stays, he or she says 안녕히 가세요 to the person who leaves. When a person leaves, he or she says 안녕히 계세요 to the person who stays.

Grammar

▶ Choose the correct answer as shown in the example below. (1~3)

이름이 뭐예요?

Ex.   저는 폴(예요. /(이에요.))   1   저는 지나(예요. / 이에요.)

2   저는 제임스(예요. / 이에요.)   3   저는 앤(예요. / 이에요.)

▶ Complete the sentence as shown in the example below. (4~6)

어느 나라 사람이에요?

Ex. 저는 __호주__ 사람이에요.

4   저는_____사람이에요.

5   저는_____.

6   _____.

▶ Complete the conversation. (7~8)

7   A   이름이 _____예요?

   B   민수예요.

8   A   _____ 사람이에요?

   B   한국 사람이에요.

▶ Listen and correctly match the name and nationality. (9~11)

Track 046

사람?	이름?	어느 나라 사람?

9 •

• ⓐ 유웨이 •

• ㉠ 영국 사람

10 •

• ⓑ 인호 •

• ㉡ 중국 사람

11 •

• ⓒ 제임스 •

• ㉢ 한국 사람

Reading

▶ Read and choose the correct answer to complete the conversation.

12

> A 안녕하세요?
>
> B 안녕하세요? 이름이 뭐예요?
>
> A 저는 제인이에요.
>
> B _____
>
> A 캐나다 사람이에요.

ⓐ 안녕하세요?

ⓑ 안녕히 가세요.

ⓒ 이름이 뭐예요?

ⓓ 어느 나라 사람이에요?

Answers p.275

A Word on Culture

Q **When meeting a Korean for the first time, what should I call him or her?**

In Korea, the word "you" is almost never used between two people, particularly the first time they meet. If you look up "you" in an English-Korean dictionary, you'll find the word 당신, but to use this term to a stranger would be considered highly discourteous. You have probably felt, upon meeting someone new, perplexed about what to call him or her. In Korea, people are addressed by titles based on age and position, which are complex even for Koreans!

For example, if you meet someone with whom you have a working relationship, you might call him by his title of 사장 (president, director) or 부장 (manager); but you would also attach 님 at the end of the title (사장님 or 부장님) to indicate respect. Now you might understand the reason Koreans almost always exchange business cards upon first meeting as these cards contain each person's appropriate title.

However, if you should happen to meet someone who does not have a prestigious occupation, after asking for his name, you may call him by his full name or first name plus 씨 at the end to indicate respect. For example, 김진수, which consists of last name 김 and first name 진수, would be called 김진수 씨 or 진수 씨. If the person you are meeting is a very close personal friend or a child, in a one-to-one conversation you can use 너 (a very informal "you"). But even if this person is an adult far younger than yourself, you cannot use 너 unless you are very close friends.

Chapter 2 아니요, 회사원이에요.

- 네 "yes" and 아니요 "no"
- Leaving out the subject of a sentence
- Asking questions
- Languages

폴 씨, 학생이에요?
Paul, are you a student?

네, 학생이에요.
Yes, I am a student.

● 네 "yes" and 아니요 "no"

Yes / no questions can be answered affirmatively with 네 and negatively with 아니요.

1 A 제인 씨, 선생님이에요?   Jane, are you a teacher?

   B 네.   Yes.

2 A 링링 씨, 학생이에요?   Lingling, are you a student?

   B 아니요, 저는 의사예요.   No, I am a doctor.

● Leaving out the subject of a sentence

In Korean, rather than repeating the subject of the sentence, if the subject is understood you can leave it out.

   A 어느 나라 사람이에요?   Which country are you from?

   B (저는) 호주 사람이에요.   I am Australian.

However, when changing the topic, do not leave the subject out of the first sentence.

   A 저는 한국 사람이에요.   I am Korean.

      제임스 씨, 어느 나라 사람이에요?   James, which country are you from?

   B (저는) 영국 사람이에요.   I am British.

리에 씨, 회사원이에요?
Rie, are you an office worker?

아니요, **일본어** 선생님이에요.
No, I am a Japanese teacher.

Asking questions

Think of questions and answers such as: "Who is he?" "He is Paul." In English, questions and answers have different structures. Verbs, subjects, and objects move around depending on the context.

In Korean, however, the word order of an answer is the same as the word order of the question. When answering a question, simply replace the question word (which, where, when, who, what, how) with your answer, keeping the original sentence structure. With yes/no questions, the question and answer can be exactly the same in structure, but the intonation is different – all questions end with a rising tone.

1	A	마크 씨, 회사원이에요?	Mark, are you an office worker?
	B	네, 저는 회사원이에요.	Yes, I am an office worker.
2	A	마크 씨, 어느 나라 사람이에요?	Mark, which country are you from?
	B	미국 사람이에요.	I am American.

Languages

Names of languages are formed by placing 말 or 어 (literally, meaning language) after the name of the country. The only difference is that 말 is more informal, while 어 is more formal. English, however, is just 영어 without referring to a country.

Country	한국 Korea	일본 Japan	중국 China	미국 U.S.A.	외국 Foreign country
Language	한국어 한국말 Korean	일본어 일본말 Japanese	중국어 중국말 Chinese	영어 English	외국어 외국말 Foreign language

Be careful

영어 (O)
영어말 (X)

Yujin	Mark, are you a student?
Mark	No.
Yujin	Then, are you a teacher?
Mark	No.
Yujin	Then, are you an office worker?
Mark	Yes. Correct. I am an office worker.

유진　마크 씨, 학생이에요?

마크　아니요.

유진　그럼, 선생님이에요?

마크　아니요.

유진　그럼, 회사원이에요?

마크　네, 맞아요. 회사원이에요.

New Vocabulary

학생 student
그럼 then, so (if so)
선생님 teacher
회사원 office worker

New Expressions

아니요. No.
네. Yes.
맞아요. Correct.

Conversation Tips

★ 그럼 "then"
When asking a question to change a topic, 그럼 is usually followed by a pause. 그럼 is a frequently used short form of 그러면.

★ Two ways to say "Yes"
When answering affirmatively, you can say 네 or 예. 예 gives a more polite impression. 네 is more frequently used.

Track 048

Jane	Jinsu, what kind of work do you do?
Jinsu	I am an office worker. Jane, are you a student?
Jane	No.
Jinsu	Then, what kind of work do you do?
Jane	I'm an English teacher.
Jinsu	Oh, really?

제인 진수 씨, 무슨 일 해요?

진수 저는 회사원이에요.

제인 씨, 학생이에요?

제인 아니요.

진수 그럼, 무슨 일 해요?

제인 영어 선생님이에요.

진수 아, 그래요?

New Vocabulary

무슨 what kind of
일 work
해요 (I) do
영어 English

New Expressions

무슨 일 해요?
What kind of work do you do?
아, 그래요? Oh, really?

Conversation Tips

★ **The meaning of the honorific 님**

The 님 in 선생님 is an honorific. In Korea, 님 is attached to many jobs and titles to indicate respect. In particular, in the workplace where rank and status are clear, a subordinate will call a superior not by his/her name but rather by a title such as 사장님 (사장 the president of a company + 님 honorific). Usually you do not add the honorific 님 when referring to your own title/job.

★ **아, 그래요? "Oh, really?/Oh, is that right?/Oh yeah?"**

This phrase is not a serious question, but a polite way to show your interest and attention, like the phrases "Oh, really?/Oh, is that right?/Oh yeah?" in English. Depending on nuance, this phrase can have many different meanings. In this case, it is written like a question, but the meaning is not really a question, so your tone should not rise too much at the end.

● 감사합니다 [감사함니다]

When a '¬, ㄷ, ㅂ' final consonant is followed by an initial consonant 'ㄴ, ㅁ', the '¬, ㄷ, ㅂ' is pronounced as [ㅇ, ㄴ, ㅁ] accordingly.

(1) ¬ → [ㅇ] 한국말 [한궁말], 부엌문 [부엉문]

(2) ㄷ → [ㄴ] 닫는 [단는], 씻는 [씬는]

(3) ㅂ → [ㅁ] 미안합니다 [미안함니다], 앞문 [암문]

Additional Vocabulary

Track 050

① ② ③ ④ ⑤ ⑥ ⑦ ⑧ ⑨ ⑩

1	학생	student
2	선생님	teacher
3	회사원	office worker
4	의사	doctor
5	간호사	nurse
6	택시 기사	taxi driver
7	주부	housewife
8	운동선수	athlete
9	경찰	policeman
10	군인	military personnel

교수(님)	professor
신부(님)	priest
수녀(님)	nun
목사(님)	pastor
변호사	lawyer
스님	monk
번역가	translator
통역사	interpreter

Track 051

In Korea, greetings differ depending on the formality of the situation and the age or status of the person you are greeting.

Greetings

A Hello.
When greeting someone older than you.
For example, parents, grandparents.

A Hello.
B Hello.
When greeting a stranger, or greeting someone you know but need to speak politely to.
For example, teachers, older neighbors, strangers, co-workers.

A Hello.
B Hello.
When greeting a friend of the same age (especially a friend from youth).
For example, childhood friends, school friends.

A Hello.
B Hello.
When meeting someone of higher status, or with whom you have a working relationship.
For example, a boss, customers.

Grammar

▶ Look at the picture and choose the correct answer. (1~2)

1　A　제임스 씨예요?

　　B　(네 / 아니요), 제임스예요.

　　A　미국 사람이에요?

　　B　(네 / 아니요), 영국 사람이에요.

제임스

2　A　리에 씨예요?

　　B　(네 / 아니요), 메이예요.

　　A　중국 사람이에요?

　　B　(네 / 아니요), 중국 사람이에요.

메이

▶ Look at the picture and complete the conversation. (3~4)

3　A　러시아어 선생님이에요?

　　B　아니요, ＿＿＿＿＿＿ 선생님이에요.

4　A　중국어 선생님이에요?

　　B　아니요, ＿＿＿＿＿＿ 선생님이에요.

▶ Connect each question to its answer. (5~7)

5　학생이에요?　　•　　　　　•　ⓐ 영어 선생님이에요.

6　무슨 일 해요?　　•　　　　　•　ⓑ 아니요, 캐나다 사람이에요.

7　미국 사람이에요?　　•　　　　　•　ⓒ 네, 학생이에요.

Listening

▶ Listen and choose the correct answer. (8~9)

Track 052

8 제인 씨가 무슨 일 해요?

    ⓐ 선생님   ⓑ 학생   ⓒ 의사   ⓓ 회사원

9 민호 씨가 무슨 일 해요?

    ⓐ 한국어 선생님   ⓑ 영어 선생님

    ⓒ 중국어 선생님   ⓓ 일본어 선생님

Reading

▶ Read and choose the correct answer to complete the conversation.

10

> A 톰 씨, 선생님이에요?
>
> B 아니요.
>
> A 그럼, (1) _____
>
> B 네, 회사원이에요.
>
>   유미 씨, 무슨 일 해요?
>
> A (2) _____

(1) ⓐ 이름이 뭐예요?

     ⓑ 회사원이에요?

     ⓒ 미국 사람이에요?

     ⓓ 어느 나라 사람이에요?

(2) ⓐ 의사예요.

     ⓑ 일본 사람이에요.

     ⓒ 네, 학생이에요.

     ⓓ 아니요, 한국 사람이에요.

Answers p.275 and p.276

A Word on Culture

Q Why do Koreans ask each other's age upon first meeting?

You may be taken aback if you're a Westerner and you see Koreans abruptly ask each other's age upon first meeting. If you're not accustomed to this practice, your inclination may be to firmly reply, "That's none of your business!" But in Korean, the reason for asking is to decide what level of speech to use with one another. The way one person speaks to another depends on whether the other person is older or younger.

In a close relationship – with a family member, neighbor, or classmate, for instance – if the person to whom you are speaking is older than you, you need to use the honorific form -(으)세요. Even if that person is not older, if you are meeting for the first time, you should use the honorific to show respect.

However, if you are similar in age or status and you wish to indicate a certain degree of closeness, you can use the polite form -아/어요. This form is most often used when buying things in a market or when asking something of someone on the street.

Casual speech (from -아/어요, the 요 is left off) is used if two people are very close, for instance with close childhood friends, when speaking to a young child or a younger sibling. Casual speech assumes closeness, so you can only use it if you have a close relationship with or receive consent from the other person, especially if you are speaking with an adult, even if he or she is younger than you. These days, due to Western influence, young people may not ask each other's age. Still, for the most part in Korea, having a conversation with someone requires the age question.

Chapter 3 이게 뭐예요?

- 이, 그, 저 "this, that, that"
- The question words 무슨 "that kind of" and 누구 "who, whose"
- The subject marker 이/가
- Possessives

이게 무슨 책이에요?
What kind of book is this?

한국어 책이에요.
This is a Korean book.

● 이, 그, 저 "this, that, that"

Appendix p.268

Like "this" and "that" in English, deciding whether to use 이, 그, or 저 depends on where an object is located relative to the speaker and listener, and whether the speaker and listener can see the object. Use 이 like "this" for an object close by. Use 그 like "that" for something near the listener but not near the speaker. Also use 그 for something that can't be seen. Use 저 like "that" for an object far away from both speaker and listener.

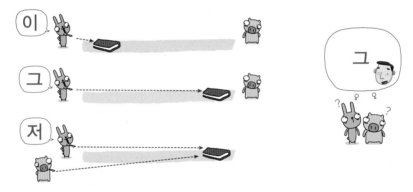

When speaking, the shortened forms of 이것이, 그것이, 저것이 "this thing, that thing, that thing" are 이게, 그게, 저게.

● The question word 무슨 "what kind of"

When trying to ask about details or characteristics about something, use the question word 무슨 followed by the noun you want to know more about.

A 저게 무슨 영화예요?   What kind of movie is that?

B 코미디 영화예요.   It's a comedy.

The subject marker 이/가

In Korean, the subject of a sentence is designated by a subject marker 이/가.

ending in a vowel	ending in a consonant
마크 씨가 미국 사람이에요. Mark is American.	선생님이 한국 사람이에요. The teacher is Korean.

Possessives

In Korean, possession is expressed by adding the marker 의 after the possessor. The marker 의 can be omitted in colloquial speech.

Student's book → 학생 책

? I wonder...
학생 책 [colloquial] = 학생의 책 [formal writing]

In the first person, my possession begins with 제, our possession begins with 우리.

My friend → 제 친구   Our school → 우리 학교

The question word 누구 "who, whose"

The question word 누구 is both the English equivalent of "who"and "whose". When asking "who" someone is, use 누구 with -예요. When asking who something belongs to (whose), place 누구 in front of the possessed noun.

A 제임스 씨가 누구예요?   Who is James?

B 저분이 제임스 씨예요.   That person is James.

A 이게 누구 가방이에요?   Whose bag is this?

B 제니 씨 가방이에요.   It is Jenny's bag.

이게 뭐예요?

숟가락이에요.

Paul	What is this?
Jina	It is a spoon.
Paul	Then, what is this?
Jina	This is rice.
Paul	Then, what is that?
Jina	It is water.

폴   이게 뭐예요?

지나   숟가락이에요.

폴   그럼, 이게 뭐예요?

지나   밥이에요.

폴   그럼, 저게 뭐예요?

지나   물이에요.

New Vocabulary

이게 this
숟가락 spoon
밥 rice, meal
저게 that
물 water

New Expressions

이게 뭐예요? What is this?
저게 뭐예요? What is that?

Conversation Tips

★ 이게 뭐예요? "What is this?"
Many English speakers will try to emphasize 뭐 as they would stress the word "what" in English. But this sounds strange in Korean. However, as with all questions, your tone should not rise at 뭐 but rather at the end.

★ 이게, 그게, 저게 "this, that, that"
These are often used in their shortened forms. 이, 그, 저 plus the noun 것 (thing) and the subject marker 이 become 이것이, 그것이, 저것이, which are then shortened to 이게, 그게, 저게. 이건, 그건, 저건 share the same meaning but with a slight emphasis on the object indicated (as they are formed from 이것, 그것, 저것 and the topic marker 은).

이게 뭐예요?	What is this? [informal]	이건 뭐예요?	What is this? [informal]
= 이것이 무엇입니까?	What is this? [formal]	= 이것은 무엇입니까?	What is this? [formal]

Rie	What is this?
Jinsu	It is a book.
Rie	What kind of book is it?
Jinsu	It is a Korean book.
Rie	Whose is it?
Jinsu	It is Mark's.
Rie	Who is Mark?
Jinsu	He is my friend.

리에 　이게 뭐예요?

진수 　책이에요.

리에 　무슨 책이에요?

진수 　한국어 책이에요.

리에 　누구 거예요?

진수 　마크 씨 거예요.

리에 　마크 씨가 누구예요?

진수 　제 친구예요.

Conversation Tips

★ **The question words 무슨 "what kind of " and 어느 "which"**
무슨 asks about something's characteristics, where as 어느 is asking someone to make a choice among multiple things.

1 A 이게 <u>무슨</u> 책이에요?
   What kind of book is this?

   B 역사 책이에요. It's a history book.

2 A 역사 책이 <u>어느</u> 책이에요?
   Which book is the history book?

   B 노란색 책이에요. It's the yellow book.

★ **누구 거예요? "Whose is it?"**
When asking about possession, "누구 거예요?" is the same as asking "누구 책이에요?" Here, 거 substitutes for 책. 거 is used in colloquial speech, while 것 is used more in writing.

● 책상 [책쌍]

When a final consonant '¬, ⊏, ㅂ' is followed by a initial consonant '¬, ⊏, ㅂ, ㅅ, ㅈ' the initial consonant is pronounced as [ㄲ, ㄸ, ㅃ, ㅆ, ㅉ] accordingly.

(1) ¬ → [ㄲ] 숟가락 [숟까락]

(2) ⊏ → [ㄸ] 먹다 [먹따]

(3) ㅂ → [ㅃ] 어젯밤 [어젣빰]

(4) ㅅ → [ㅆ] 통역사 [통역싸]

(5) ㅈ → [ㅉ] 걱정 [걱쩡]

Additional Vocabulary

Track 056

1	열쇠	key
2	휴지	tissue
3	핸드폰	cell phone
4	시계	watch
5	안경	glasses
6	여권	passport
7	우산	umbrella
8	칫솔	toothbrush
9	치약	toothpaste
10	거울	mirror
11	빗	comb

12	돈	money
13	운전면허증	driver's license
14	사진	photo
15	명함	business card
16	외국인 등록증	foreigner's registration card

Track 057

Asking questions

A   What is this in English?

A   How do you say this in Korean?

Responding to others

A   I don't understand.

A   I understand.

Grammar

▶ Choose the correct answer to complete the sentence. (1~4)

1 선생님(이 / 가) 한국 사람이에요.   2 사토루(이 / 가) 일본 사람이에요.

3 폴(이 / 가) 호주 사람이에요.   4 마크(이 / 가) 미국 사람이에요.

▶ Look at the picture and complete the conversation. (5~6)

5   A 이분이 누구예요?

   B _____ 씨예요.

   마크

6   A 이분이 누구예요?

   B _____.

   제인

(＊분 is the honorific form of 사람)

▶ Look at the picture and complete the conversation as in the example. (7~8)

Ex. A 이게 뭐예요?

     B _____열쇠예요_____.

     A 누구 거예요?

     B _____폴 씨_____ 거예요.

7 A 저게 뭐예요?

   B (1) _____.

   A 누구 거예요?

   B (2) _____ 거예요.

유진

8 A (1) _____ 뭐예요?

   B 안경이에요.

   A (2) _____ 거예요?

   B 유웨이 씨 거예요.

유웨이

Listening

▶ Look at the picture. Listen and choose the correct answer.

9 이게 뭐예요?

    ⓐ   ⓑ   ⓒ   ⓓ

▶ Listen and choose the correct answer to complete the conversation.

10 A 가방이 누구 거예요?

   B _____.

ⓐ   ⓑ   ⓒ   ⓓ

Reading

▶ Read and complete the conversation based on the given question. (11~12)

> 뭐예요?   누구예요?   누구 거예요?   무슨 일 해요?

11 A 이분이 (1) _____

   B 제임스 씨예요.

   A 제임스 씨는 (2) _____

   B 영어 선생님이에요.

12 A 이게 (1) _____

   B 여권이에요.

   A (2) _____

   B 제임스 씨 거예요.

Answers p.276

A Word on Culture

Q **Have you heard the phrases 우리 나라 and 우리 집?**

You've probably noticed that Koreans use the term 우리 "our" quite often: 우리 나라 "my country" (lit. our country), 우리 회사 "my company" (lit. our company), 우리 집 "my house" (lit. our house), 우리 남편 "my husband" (lit. our husband), 우리 엄마 "my mother" (lit. our mother), etc. It's not because everyone has multiple personality disorder or that there is joint ownership of everything!

The use of this term emphasizes community over individuality. When expressing possession, Koreans will often say "our" in order to stress their affiliations, rather than saying "my," which expresses individuality. Terms such as 우리 나라 and 우리 회사 consciously or unconsciously reinforce a sense of unity. In daily life, Koreans prefer to do even trivial things together, rather than do things alone. Koreans dislike having even a light meal or coffee alone. Koreans feel safer and happier when together and feel that activities done together strengthen relationships. This is the reason you will rarely find someone eating or drinking alone in a restaurant in Korea.

Despite how much Koreans like to use "our," the term can't be used all the time. When it's necessary to show possession of something by an individual, the possessive "my" is used. To say "our bag" or "our cell phone," for instance, would be very odd.

It may feel strange at first to use the collective "our," but like spicy Kimchi, repeated use can acclimate your tongue to it.

Chapter 4 화장실이 어디에 있어요?

- 있어요 "there is(are)" and 없어요 "there is(are) not"
- The place marker 에
- The question word 어디 "where"
- Location-based expressions

마크 씨가 **어디**에 있어요?
Where is Mark?

사무실에 **있어요.**
He is in the office.

● **있어요** "there is(are)" **and 없어요** "there is(are) not"
Appendix p.267

Use 있어요 when something exists, 없어요 when something does not. Place the subject marker 이 / 가 after the noun which exists (or not) and then 있어요, 없어요.

의자가 있어요.	There is a chair.
의자가 없어요.	There is no chair.

● **The place marker 에**

Putting the place marker 에 after a noun indicates a spatial location.

폴이 공원에 있어요.	Paul is at the park.
= 공원에 폴이 있어요.	

It doesn't matter whether the object is specified before or after the location, or vice versa. As with all verbs, 있어요 and 없어요 always come at the end of a sentence.

● **The question word 어디** "where"

Using 어디, followed by the place marker 에 with the verb 있어요 allows you to ask where something is located.

A	선생님이 어디에 있어요?	Where is the teacher?
B	(선생님이) 학교에 있어요.	The teacher is at school.

Location-based expressions

책상 위에

on the desk

책상 아래에

under the desk

의자 앞에

in front of the chair

의자 뒤에

behind the chair

시계 옆에

next to the clock

컵 오른쪽에

to the right of the cup

컵 왼쪽에

to the left of the cup

컵하고 시계 사이에

between the cup and the clock

냉장고 안에

inside the refrigerator

냉장고 밖에

outside of the refrigerator

> **! Be careful**
>
> Use 제 when describing as object's position to yourself, but use 저 with 하고.
>
> 의자가 제 앞에 있어요.
> The chair is in front of me.
>
> 의자가 제 오른쪽에 있어요.
> The chair is to the right of me.
>
> 의자가 저하고 책상 사이에 있어요.
> The chair is between me and the desk.

Paul	Excuse me, is there a bathroom near here?
Mei	Yes, there is.
Paul	Where is it?
Mei	Over there, next to the vending machine.
Paul	Thank you.
Mei	You're welcome.

폴　저, 이 근처에 화장실 있어요?

메이　네, 있어요.

폴　어디에 있어요?

메이　저기 자판기 옆에 있어요.

폴　감사합니다.

메이　네.

New Vocabulary

이 this
근처 vicinity
화장실 bathroom
있어요 there is
어디에 where
저기 over there
자판기 vending machine
옆 beside

New Expressions

저 Excuse me.
이 근처에 … 있어요?
Is there … near here?
어디에 있어요? Where is it?
감사합니다. Thank you.
네. You're welcome.

Conversation Tips

★ 저 "Excuse me."

저 is a polite way to get someone's attention in order to ask them something. You can use it with someone nearby who you don't know. 저 is followed by a small pause to allow the person to pay attention, and then you can begin your conversation. 저기요 is also used this way.

★ The various meanings of 네

When answering affirmatively, you can say 네. Also, 네 is often used to mean "sure" or "you're welcome" when communicating with a stranger or in formal situations in order to convey politeness.

Track 061

집이 어디에 있어요?

Yujin	Mark, where is your house?
Mark	It's in Sinchon.
Yujin	Where in Sinchon?
Mark	Do you know Sinchon pharmacy?
Yujin	No, I don't.
Mark	Then do you know Sinchon department store?
Yujin	Yes, I do.
Mark	My house is right behind Sinchon department store.

유진 마크 씨, 집이 어디에 있어요?

마크 신촌에 있어요.

유진 신촌 어디에 있어요?

마크 신촌 약국 알아요?

유진 아니요, 몰라요.

마크 그럼, 신촌 백화점 알아요?

유진 네, 알아요.

마크 신촌 백화점 바로 뒤에 있어요.

New Vocabulary

집 house

신촌 Sinchon (area of Seoul)

약국 pharmacy

알아요 I know

몰라요 I don't know

백화점 department store

바로 right, just

뒤 behind

New Expressions

··· 알아요? Do you know···?

신촌 어디에 있어요?
Where in Sinchon?

바로 뒤에 있어요.
It is right behind.

Conversation Tips

★ 신촌 어디에 있어요? "Where in Sinchon?"
This pattern is used when you are trying to find a more exact location. The area you're asking about is followed by the phrase 어디에 있어요?.

★ 바로 "right, just, precisely, exactly"
Used for emphasis; place 바로 right in front of the word you want to emphasize.

● 없어요 [업써요]

Sometimes a word (such as 없) contains a double final consonant. If the second final consonant is '人' and it is followed by a vowel (as in 없어요), this '人' is pronounced as a strong [ㅆ] sound in the next syllable. So 없어요 is pronounced as [업써요].

(1) 값이 [갑씨]

(2) 몫이에요 [목씨에요]

Additional Vocabulary

Track 063

1	집	house
2	편의점	convenience store
3	은행	bank
4	병원	hospital
5	학교	school
6	약국	pharmacy
7	영화관	movie theater
8	헬스장	gym
9	식당	restaurant

회사	company
가게	store
시장	market
주차장	parking lot
주유소	gas station
대사관	embassy
공항	airport
공원	park
서점	bookstore
우체국	post office
카페	café

In Korean, the same things may be said in different ways, depending on the situation and whom you are talking to.

Saying thanks

A Thank you.

B You're welcome.

When speaking politely in a formal situation.
For instance, to a customer, a person who is older than you, or a stranger.

A Thank you.

B It's nothing.

When speaking politely in a semi-formal situation.
For instance, to a close co-worker.

A Thanks.

B Don't mention it.

When speaking friendly in an informal situation.
For instance, to a classmate or a childhood friend.

Grammar

▶ Look at the picture and complete the conversation. (1~4)

1   A 폴 씨가 어디에 있어요?

   B _____에 있어요.

2   A 앤 씨가 어디에 있어요?

   B _____에 있어요.

3   A 인호 씨가 어디에 있어요?

   B _____ 있어요.

4   A 리에 씨가 어디에 있어요?

   B _____.

▶ Complete the conversation. (5~6)

5   A 마크 씨가 _____ 있어요?

   B 공원에 있어요.

6   A 제인 씨가 _____?

   B 병원에 있어요.

▶ Look at the picture and complete the conversation. (7~9)

7   A 시계가 어디에 있어요?

   B 책상 _____에 있어요.

8   A 책이 어디에 있어요?

   B 안경 _____에 있어요.

9   A 안경이 어디에 있어요?

   B 책하고 시계 _____에 있어요.

▶ Look at the picture. Listen and choose the correct answer.

10 　ⓐ　　　　ⓑ　　　　ⓒ　　　　ⓓ

Track 065

▶ Listen and choose the correct answer.

Track 066

11　책이 어디에 있어요?

ⓐ 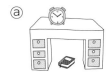　ⓑ 　ⓒ 　ⓓ

Reading

▶ Look at the picture. Read and choose the correct answer.

폴 씨 집 근처에 빌딩이 많이 있어요. 폴 씨 집 옆에 식당이 있어요.
폴 씨 집 앞에 병원이 있어요. 폴 씨 집 오른쪽에 편의점이 있어요.
그런데 폴 씨 집 옆에 은행이 없어요.

12　폴 씨 집이 어디에 있어요?　(　　　　　　　)

Answers p.276

A Word on Culture

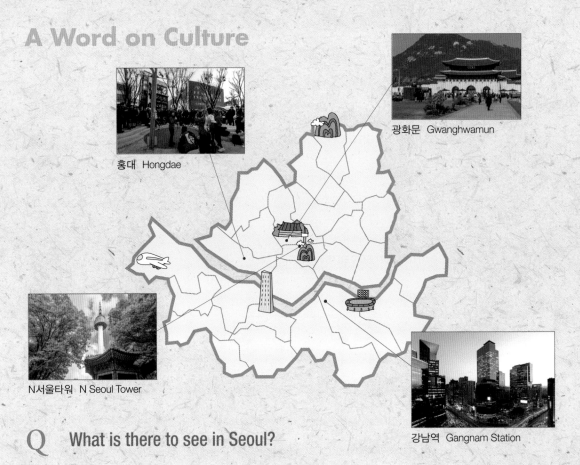

홍대 Hongdae

광화문 Gwanghwamun

N서울타워 N Seoul Tower

강남역 Gangnam Station

Q   What is there to see in Seoul?

Seoul, the capital of Korea, consists of 20% of the total Korean population, is a metropolis with a 600-year history, and has a variety of features that offers many different things to see. First, if you want to feel the history of Koreja, it is recommended to view the beauty of the Chosun Dynasty palaces in the city center. The quiet and still atmosphere of the palace among the modern buildings is quite attractive. It is also good to enjoy a cup of tea in Insadong, a district where traditional crafts and tea houses are gathered. If you go to N Seoul Tower, located in the center of Seoul, you can see downtown Seoul in a single glance. In particular, you can see the breathtaking night view of Seoul at night. The Han River Park can be found along the Han River that runs through the middle of Seoul. Here, you can spot Seoulites who are taking a break, walking, or eating delivery meals. There are over 100 large and small mountains in Seoul which many people enjoy climbing. You can enjoy the nature of Seoul's mountains as it is conveniently connected by way of subway. If you want to experience a youthful atmosphere, you can find various trending fashion, busking, or indie band performances in Hongdae. If you want to feel the modern urban atmosphere, you can enjoy various cultural performances and good food/drinks in Gangnam. If you like shopping, you can experience the latest trends in Myeongdong or Hongdae, and the bargaining of traditional markets in Namdaemun Market or Dongdaemun Market. As a bonus, there are various festivals and exhibitions throughout Seoul! Moreover, Seoul is a city that is awake 24 hours. Are you ready to enjoy what Seoul has to offer?

Chapter 5 동생이 몇 명 있어요?

- 있어요 "have" and 없어요 "don't have"
- Native Korean numbers
- Counting words
- The question word 몇 "how many"

동생 **있어요?**
Do you have any younger siblings?

네, 두 명 있어요.
Yes, I have two.

있어요 "have" and 없어요 "don't have"

In the last chapter we saw that 있어요 and 없어요 can indicate existence. In this chapter you will see how 있어요 and 없어요 is also used to indicate what someone possesses. After the subject comes the object, and then 있어요 is used at the end of sentence. 없어요 is used to indicate what someone doesn't have.

마크가 집이 있어요.   Mark has a house.

마크가 자동차가 없어요.   Mark doesn't have a car.

? I wonder...

Note that in the examples, "house" and "car" are objects in English. But in Korean, when you use the verb 있어요 and 없어요, these possessive objects always take the marker 이/가.

Native Korean numbers

Korean has two systems of numbers – a native Korean number system and a number system that has its roots in Chinese, called Sino-Korean numbers. When counting objects, use native Korean numbers.

1	하나	11	열하나	30	서른
2	둘	12	열둘	40	마흔
3	셋	13	열셋	50	쉰
4	넷	14	열넷	60	예순
5	다섯	15	열다섯	70	일흔
6	여섯	16	열여섯	80	여든
7	일곱	17	열일곱	90	아흔
8	여덟	18	열여덟	100	백
9	아홉	19	열아홉		
10	열	20	스물		

Counting words

Appendix p.264

When counting objects or the number of people, state the object first, the native Korean number next, and then a counting word last. This counting word changes depending upon the object that is being counted (refer to page 264 for a list of counting words).

   five cups → 컵 5 (다섯) 개

Korean numbers 1~4 and 20 change forms a bit before counting words.

     two clocks → 시계 2 (두) 개

하나	→	한 개
둘	→	두 개
셋	→	세 개
넷	→	네 개
다섯	→	다섯 개
⋮		⋮
스물	→	스무 개

The question word 몇 "how many"

몇 is the question word for "how many," used for asking about the number of things. Always use the appropriate counting word after 몇 and before the verb.

A 표가 몇 장 있어요?   How many tickets do you have?

B (표가) 두 장 있어요.   I have two tickets.

Track 067

우산 있어요?

있어요.

Jinsu	Jane, do you have an umbrella?
Jane	Yes, I do.
Jinsu	How many umbrellas do you have?
Jane	I have two umbrellas. Do you have an umbrella?
Jinsu	No, I do not.
Jane	Really? Here is an umbrella.
Jinsu	Thank you.

진수   제인 씨, 우산 있어요?

제인   네, 있어요.

진수   우산이 몇 개 있어요?

제인   우산이 두 개 있어요.

       진수 씨는 우산이 있어요?

진수   아니요, 없어요.

제인   그래요? 우산 여기 있어요.

진수   감사합니다.

New Vocabulary

우산 umbrella
있어요 (I) have
몇 how many
개 unit counter
두 two
여기 here

New Expressions

우산 있어요?
Do you have an umbrella?

우산이 몇 개 있어요?
How many umbrellas do you have?

여기 있어요.
Here it is.

Conversation Tips

★ **The marker 이/가 is omitted when asking question**
"우산이 있어요." is a sentence in which the subject is omitted, and the marker 이/가 and 있어요 are combined. However, when asking a question in casual speech, it is more natural to omit the marker 이/가 before 있어요.

★ **The marker 은/는**
The marker 은/는 is a marker that is used to indicate the topic. When the topic of the conversation changes from Jane to Jinsu, the marker 은/는 is added after the noun indicating a change in the subject.

A   한국어 책 있어요?   Do you have a Korean book?
B   아니요, 없어요. 마크 씨는 한국어책 있어요?   No, I don't. Mark, do you have a Korean book?
     네, 있어요.   Yes, I do.

Conversation_2

Rie	Mark, do you have any younger siblings?
Mark	Yes, I do.
Rie	How many younger siblings do you have?
Mark	I have two.
Rie	Then, do you also have an older brother?
Mark	No, I don't.
Rie	Then, how many people are in your family all together?
Mark	My parents and me and two younger siblings, five all together.

리에   마크 씨, 동생 있어요?

마크   네, 있어요.

리에   동생이 몇 명 있어요?

마크   두 명 있어요.

리에   그럼, 형도 있어요?

마크   아니요, 없어요.

리에   그럼, 가족이 모두 몇 명이에요?

마크   부모님하고 저하고 동생 두 명, 모두
　　　다섯 명이에요.

New Vocabulary

동생 younger sibling

명 counter for people

형 older brother (of a man)

도 also

가족 family

모두 all together, in total (referring only to people)

부모님 parents

하고 and (used between nouns)

다섯 five (the native Korean number)

New Expressions

동생이 몇 명 있어요?
How many younger siblings do you have?

가족이 모두 몇 명이에요?
How many people are in your family all together?

Conversation Tips

★ **가족이 몇 명이에요? "How many people are in your family?"**
This question is the same as "가족이 몇 명 있어요?"; both ask how many people are in your family.
"가족이 몇 명이에요?" is a bit more natural.

★ **도 "also"**
Use 도 after a noun to mean "too" or "also." 도 replaces the marker 이/가.

A   한국 친구가 10명쯤 있어요.　I have about 10 Korean friends.
B   그럼, 중국 친구도 있어요?　Then, do you also have Chinese friends?

● 몇 개[멷 깨], 몇 명[면 명]

몇 is by rule pronounced as [멷]. This causes the following pronunciation changes:

1. When the final consonant sound [ㄷ] in 몇 is followed by the initial consonant 'ㄱ, ㄷ, ㅂ, ㅅ, ㅈ' in the next syllable, the 'ㄱ, ㄷ, ㅂ, ㅅ, ㅈ' are pronounced as [ㄲ, ㄸ, ㅃ, ㅆ, ㅉ] accordingly (see chapter 3).

   몇 살 [멷 쌀], 몇 잔 [멷 짠]

2. The final consonant sound [ㄷ] in 몇 is pronounced as a [ㄴ] sound before the initial consonants 'ㄴ' or 'ㅁ' in the next syllable (see chapter 2).

   몇 마리 [면 마리], 몇 마디 [면 마디]

Additional Vocabulary

Track 070

1 할아버지	grandfather	오빠	(female's) elder brother	고모	paternal aunt
2 할머니	grandmother	언니	(female's) elder sister	이모	maternal aunt
3 아버지	father	남편	husband	삼촌	paternal uncle
4 어머니	mother	부인	someone's wife	외삼촌	maternal uncle
5 형	(male's) elder brother	아내	my wife	친척	relatives
6 누나	(male's) elder sister	아들	son		
7 남동생	younger brother	딸	daughter		
8 여동생	younger sister	사촌	cousin		

Receiving guests

A May I come in?
B Yes, please come in.

A Please sit down here.
B Okay, thank you.

A Would you like to drink some coffee?
B Yes, thank you.

※ When someone offers you a drink.
A 뭐 드시겠어요? "What would you like to drink?"
B 녹차 주세요. "Please give me green tea."

A Thank you for the coffee.
B Please come again.

Quiz Yourself!

Grammar

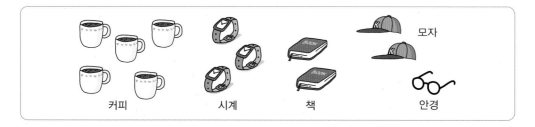

커피   시계   책   모자   안경

▶ Look at the picture and choose the correct answer. (1~4)

1   모자가 (ⓐ 있어요. / ⓑ 없어요.)   2   가방이 (ⓐ 있어요. / ⓑ 없어요.)

3   안경이 (ⓐ 있어요. / ⓑ 없어요.)   4   휴지가 (ⓐ 있어요. / ⓑ 없어요.)

▶ Look at the picture and complete the conversation. (5~7)

Ex.
A   시계가 몇 개 있어요?

B   __세__ 개 있어요.

5   A   안경이 몇 개 있어요?

    B   _____ 개 있어요.

6   A   책이 몇 권 있어요?

    B   _____ 권 있어요.

7   A   커피가 몇 잔 있어요?

    B   _____ 있어요.

▶ Look at the picture and complete the conversation. (8~9)

8

A   우산 (1)_____?

B   네, 있어요.

A   우산이 (2)_____ 있어요?

B   한 개 있어요.

9

A   한국 친구 (1)_____?

B   네, 있어요.

A   한국 친구가 (2)_____?

B   두 명 있어요.

Listening

▶ Listen and complete the sentence. (10~13)

Track 072

> Ex.   의자가 __세__ 개 있어요.

10 동생이 _____ 명 있어요.   **11** 가방이 _____ 개 있어요.

12 표가 _____ 장 있어요.   **13** 책이 _____ 권 있어요.

▶ Listen and choose the correct answer.

Track 073

14 뭐가 가방에 없어요?

ⓐ 안경   ⓑ 우산   ⓒ 지갑   ⓓ 휴지

Reading

▶ Read and complete the table.

15 제인은 친구가 몇 명 있어요?

> 저는 친구가 열 명 있어요.
> 한국 친구가 네 명, 미국 친구가 세 명, 캐나다 친구가 한 명,
> 일본 친구가 두 명이 있어요.
> 그런데 영국 친구가 없어요. 중국 친구도 없어요.

한국 친구	일본 친구	중국 친구	미국 친구	영국 친구	캐나다 친구
__4__ 명	(1)____ 명	(2)____ 명	(3)____ 명	(4)____ 명	(5)____ 명

Answers p.276 and p.277

A Word on Culture

Q Why do people use family titles like 할아버지 to refer to non-family?

As if it isn't enough that you have to worry about speaking a foreign language, in Korean you constantly have to struggle with what to call people. As a foreigner, you may be forgiven for small mistakes as long as you don't keep making them! In Korean, you must never call someone older than yourself by his or her name. Rather, you must call him or her by an appropriate familial title.

All older family members should be addressed by a title, no matter how close you are. If you are a woman, an older sister should be called 언니 and an older brother 오빠. If you are a man, your older sister should be called 누나 and your older brother should be called 형. But interestingly enough, family titles can also be used to refer to those outside your family. Since Confucian ideology sees the family as a model for society as a whole, family titles are used with non-family members to describe social relationships as well. In English, you can call anyone a "friend," but in Korean, 친구 (friend) only refers to someone your same age. An older friend (even just one year older) is not 친구 but rather 언니, 오빠, 누나 or 형 (depending on your gender and the gender of your friend).

You may refer to a 70 or 80-year-old you meet on the street as 할아버지 or 할머니. Though 아줌마 and 아저씨 used to be strictly family titles, they are now used to refer to the many 40 or 50-year-olds you may meet in the course of a day, such as taxi drivers or store owners. But be careful using these titles – they can give you a sense of intimacy, but a misuse of them can be very dissatisfying for the listener. Calling a young-looking 30-year-old woman 아줌마, for instance, might elicit a very cold response. It is similar to calling a young woman "Mrs." in Western countries! Now you understand why one of the first questions Koreans will ask upon making an acquaintance is, "How old are you?"

Chapter 6 전화번호가 몇 번이에요?

- Sino-Korean numbers
- Reading phone numbers
- The question word 몇 번 "what number"
- 이/가 아니에요 "is not … (noun)"
- How to read Sino-Korean numbers

전화번호가 **몇 번**이에요?
What is your phone number?

010-9729-8534예요.
It is 010-9729-8534.

● Sino-Korean numbers

Although native Korean numbers are used for counting, Sino-Korean numbers are used for reading numbers.

1	2	3	4	5	6	7	8	9	10
일	이	삼	사	오	육	칠	팔	구	십

● Reading phone numbers

Use Sino-Korean numbers when reading telephone numbers. Just as in English, Koreans usually read each number separately. Zero is read as 공 and the dash is read as [에].

0	1	0	-	9	7	2	9	-	8	5	3	4
공	일	공	[에]	구	칠	이	구	[에]	팔	오	삼	사

● The question word 몇 번 "what number"

몇 번 is used to ask for a number – not a quantity, but a number (for instance, phone number, driver's license number, ticket number, parking space number).

A 회사 전화번호가 몇 번이에요?　What is the phone number at your workplace?

B 6359-4278이에요.　It is 6359-4278.

● 이/가 아니에요 "is not… (noun)"

Appendix p.267

이/가 아니다 expresses that A, which is the subject of the sentence, is not noun B (A≠B). In this case, the marker 이/가 is added to B, not the sentence's subject, and expressed in the form of 'A is not B', which is combined with the sentence subject A, is sometimes replaced with the marker 은/는 and, furthermore, is occasionally omitted in colloquial speech.

ending in a vowel	ending in a consonant
(저는) 가수가 아니에요. I am not a singer.	(폴은) 선생님이 아니에요. Paul is not a teacher.

● How to read Sino-Korean numbers

thousand 천	hundred 백	ten 십	
		6 육십	7 칠
	1 백	2 이십	9 구
5 오천	3 삼백	8 팔십	4 사

! Be careful

In Korean, don't say "one" when it is the first digit as in: "one hundred", "one thousand", etc.

백 이십 구 (o) one hundred twenty−nine
일백 이십 구 (x)

Track 074

전화번호 몇 번?

잠깐만요.

Satoru	Do you happen to know Paul's phone number?
Jina	Yes, I know it.
Satoru	What's Paul's number?
Jina	Hold on. It's 010-7428-9135.
Satoru	Is 010-7428-9135 right?
Jina	Yes, that's right.
Satoru	Thanks.
Jina	You're welcome.

사토루 혹시 폴 씨 전화번호 알아요?

지나 네, 알아요.

사토루 폴 씨 전화번호가 몇 번이에요?

지나 잠깐만요. 010-7428-9135예요.

사토루 010-7428-9135 맞아요?

지나 네, 맞아요.

사토루 고마워요.

지나 아니에요.

New Vocabulary

혹시 by any chance
전화번호 phone number
몇 what
번 number
몇 번 what number

New Expressions

혹시 … 알아요?
Do you happen to know…?
전화번호가 몇 번이에요?
What is your phone number?
잠깐만요. Hold on.
맞아요. Yes.
고마워요. Thanks.
아니에요. You're welcome.

Conversation Tips

★ 혹시 "by any chance"
This is an adverb that goes at the beginning of the question to indicate a supposition. Use 아마 ("maybe") to indicate supposition in a statement.

A 혹시 앤 씨 전화번호를 알아요?
Do you happen to know Ann's phone number?

B 아마 마크 씨가 알 거예요. Maybe Mark will know it.
(We will learn the future tense in chapter 15.)

★ 고마워요."Thanks."
Use this light form of thanks in informal situations and relationships.

Track 075

Yujin	Paul, do you happen to know Mark's home phone number?
Paul	No, I don't know it. But I know his office phone number.
Yujin	What is Mark's office phone number?
Paul	Hold on. It's 6942-7143.
Yujin	Is 6942-7243 right?
Paul	No. It's not 7243. It's 7143.
Yujin	Thank you.

유진   폴 씨, 혹시 마크 씨 집 전화번호 알아요?

폴   아니요, 몰라요.
그런데 회사 전화번호는 알아요.

유진   마크 씨 회사 전화번호가 몇 번이에요?

폴   잠깐만요. 6942-7143이에요.

유진   6942-7243 맞아요?

폴   아니요. 7243이 아니에요. 7143이에요.

유진   감사합니다.

New Vocabulary

집 home
그런데 but, however
회사 company, office
은/는 contrast marker

New Expressions

7243이 아니에요.
It is not 7243.

Conversation Tips

★ **Contrast marker 은/는**
Another function of the marker 은/는 is to provide contrast, or to emphasize difference. In the example, the speaker doesn't know someone's home number, but he does know the mobile phone number.

A 집 전화번호 알아요?   Do you know his home phone number?
B 아니요, 그런데 핸드폰 번호는 알아요.   No, but I know his mobile phone number.

★ **아니요 vs. 아니에요**
아니요 means "no" when you are asked a yes/no question, as the opposite of 네 ("yes").
아니에요 means "···isn't [noun]", as the opposite of -예요/이에요 ("is [noun]"). 아니에요 needs the marker 이/가.

Ex. 1   A 의사예요?   Are you a doctor?   Ex. 2   저는 의사가 아니에요.   I'm not a doctor.
B 아니요.   No.

● **잠깐만요** [잠깐마뇨]

In Korean, when a final consonant is followed by a vowel, the final consonant moves to be pronounced as the initial consonant of the next syllable. So, 잠깐만요 should be pronounced as [잠깐마뇨], but in reality, Koreans may pronounce them as [잠깐만요]. When a word ending in a final consonant 'ㄴ, ㅁ' is followed by 이, 야, 여, 요, 유, the 'ㄴ' is pronounced as if it is added as the initial consonant of the next syllable: [니, 냐, 녀, 뇨, 뉴] accordingly.

그럼요 [그러묘]

Additional Vocabulary

Track 077

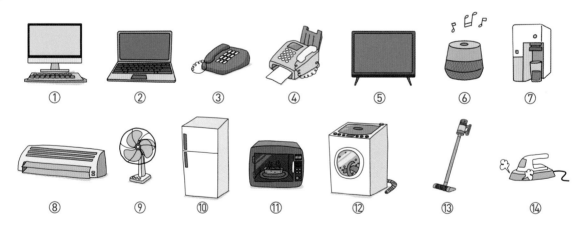

1 컴퓨터	computer	6 스피커	speaker	11 전자레인지	microwave
2 노트북	laptop	7 정수기	water purifier	12 세탁기	washing machine
3 전화(기)	phone	8 에어컨	air conditioner	13 청소기	vacuum cleaner
4 팩스	fax	9 선풍기	fan	14 다리미	iron
5 텔레비전	television	10 냉장고	refrigerator		

Phone expressions

A Hello.
B Hello.
When beginning a phone conversation.

※ When ending a phone conversation:
  안녕히 계세요. "Goodbye."

A May I speak to Mark?
B Yes, just a minute.
When asking to speak to someone on the phone.

A May I speak to Mark?
B He's not here right now.
When the person is not in.

※ When you don't know the name of the person calling:
  실례지만, 누구세요? "May I ask who's calling?"

A May I speak to Tom?
B You dialed the wrong number.
When someone calls the wrong number.

Grammar

▶ Write the correct phone number as shown in the example below. (1~2)

전화번호가 몇 번이에요?

Ex.  3542-3068 → <u>삼오사이에 삼공육팔이에요.</u>

1 6734-5842 → _____.

2 010-4328-9267 → _____.

▶ Look at the picture and complete the conversation. (3~4)

3
    A 이게 책상이에요?
    B 아니요, 책상_____ 아니에요. 의자예요.

4
    A 이게 시계예요?
    B 아니요, _____. 가방이에요.

▶ Choose the correct answer to complete the sentence. (5~6)

5 전화가 있어요. 텔레비전이 있어요. 그런데 컴퓨터(은 / 는) 없어요.

6 가방이 있어요. 책이 있어요. 그런데 지갑(은 / 는) 없어요.

Listening

▶ Listen and choose the correct answer. (7~8)

Track 079

7 병원 전화번호가 몇 번이에요?

    ⓐ 794-5269예요.

    ⓑ 794-5239예요.

    ⓒ 784-5269예요.

8 유진 씨 핸드폰 번호가 몇 번이에요?

    ⓐ 010-4539-6027이에요.

    ⓑ 010-4529-6027이에요.

    ⓒ 010-4539-8027이에요.

▶ Listen and choose the correct answer.

Track 080

9 ⓐ 폴이 핸드폰이 없어요.   ⓑ 폴이 제인 씨 집을 알아요.

  ⓒ 폴이 제인 씨 집 전화번호를 알아요.   ⓓ 폴이 제인 씨 핸드폰 번호를 알아요.

Reading

▶ Read and choose the correct answer to complete the conversation.

10

> A 혹시 제임스 씨 집 전화번호 알아요?
>
> B 아니요, (1) _____
>
> A 그럼, 제임스 씨 사무실 전화번호 알아요?
>
> B 네, 사무실 전화번호는 알아요.
>
> A 전화번호가 (2) _____
>
> B 7495-0342예요.

(1) ⓐ 알아요.

    ⓑ 몰라요.

    ⓒ 있어요.

(2) ⓐ 몇 번이에요?

    ⓑ 몇 개 있어요?

    ⓒ 몇 번 있어요?

Answers p.277

A Word on Culture

Q **Why is it that Koreans say they are a year or two older than they should be?**

As stated previously, age is very important to Koreans. In Korea, age partially determines status and shapes the way one interacts with others. So why do Koreans seem to count age differently than Westerners do?

First, because Koreans count the time that a baby spends in the womb, newborn babies are considered to be a year old at birth. In addition to that, Koreans don't think of birthdays in the same way as Westerners.

Rather, following tradition, when the old year ends and the new year begins on the morning of the Lunar New Year, everyone eats 떡국 (a soup made with rice cakes) and "eats" another year in age (Koreans say 한 살을 먹다). So, no matter when your actual birthday is, your Korean age increases on the New Year rather than your birthday. Therefore, depending on the time of year, your Korean age is 1 or 2 years older than your age by Western reckoning. This could make a big difference in age.

For example, a baby born in December meets the world at age 1 and turns 2 a month later in January. In Korea, when one needs to write down their age for formal purposes, one either writes down the date of birth (year, month, day) or calculates in the Western way, with the word 만 attached before the age. Some people who would rather knock a couple of years off their age opt to use this 만 age all the time!

Chapter 7 생일이 며칠이에요?

- Reading dates (year, month, day)
- The question words 언제 "when" and 며칠 "what day"
- 요일 Days of the week
- The time marker 에

Reading dates (year, month, day)

In Korean, dates are read with Sino-Korean numbers from the largest to the smallest unit: year first, then month, then the day last.

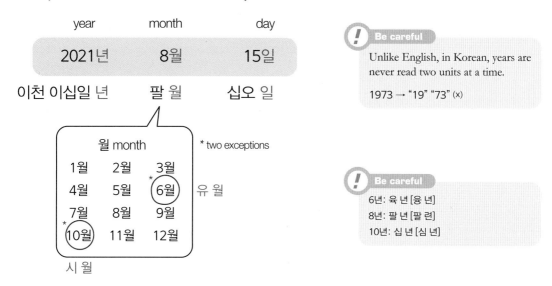

year	month	day
2021년	8월	15일
이천 이십일 년	팔 월	십오 일

월 month   * two exceptions

1월	2월	3월
4월	5월	6월 유 월
7월	8월	9월
10월	11월	12월

시 월

> **! Be careful**
>
> Unlike English, in Korean, years are never read two units at a time.
>
> 1973 → "19" "73" (x)

> **! Be careful**
>
> 6년: 육 년 [융 년]
> 8년: 팔 년 [팔 련]
> 10년: 십 년 [심 년]

The question words 언제 "when" and 며칠 "what day"

Appendix p.264

When asking what time an event will occur/occurred, 언제 is used. But, if asking specifically about a date, use 며칠.

1   A   생일이 언제예요?   When is your birthday?

    B   3월 17일이에요.   It is March 17th.

2   A   한글날이 며칠이에요?   What day is Hangeul Day?

    B   10월 9일이에요.   It is October 9th.

> **! Be careful**
>
> When asking today's date
>
> 오늘이 며칠이에요? (o)
> 오늘이 언제예요? (x)

요일 Days of the week

월요일	화요일	수요일	목요일	금요일	토요일	일요일
Monday	Tuesday	Wednesday	Thursday	Friday	Saturday	Sunday

Days of the week have to come at the end of dates.　Ex. 2021년 8월 15일 일요일

A　오늘이 무슨 요일이에요?　　What day of the week is it?

B　토요일이에요.　　It is Saturday.

The time marker 에

In Korean, times are marked by the time marker 에. Place the marker after the time.

A　언제 태권도 수업이 있어요?　When do you have Taekwondo class?

B　토요일에 있어요.　I have class on Saturday.

Use the time marker 에 only once in a sentence; place it after the smallest interval of time.

A　다음 달 15일 저녁에 시간 있어요?　Do you have time in the evening on the 15th of next month?

B　미안해요. 시간 없어요.　Sorry, I don't have time.

Track 081

Paul	Jina, what day is your birthday?
Jina	It is June 14th. Paul, when is your birthday?
Paul	It's this Friday. Do you have time on Friday?
Jina	Yes, I have time.
Paul	Then, let's eat together then.
Jina	That sounds good.

폴   지나 씨, 생일이 며칠이에요?

지나   6월 14일이에요.
      폴 씨는 생일이 언제예요?

폴   이번 주 금요일이에요.
      금요일에 시간 있어요?

지나   네, 시간 있어요.

폴   그럼, 그때 같이 식사해요.

지나   좋아요.

New Vocabulary

생일 birthday
며칠 what day
월 month
일 day
언제 when
이번 주 this week
금요일 Friday
에 the time marker
시간 time
그때 then, that day
같이 together
식사해요 (I) eat

New Expressions

생일이 며칠이에요?
What day is your birthday?

생일이 언제예요?
When is your birthday?

금요일에 시간 있어요?
Do you have time on Friday?

그때 같이 식사해요.
Let's eat together then.

좋아요. That sounds good.

Conversation Tips

★ 그때 같이 식사해요. "Let's eat together then."
같이("together") is used in this sentence to suggest that an action be done together. In informal circumstances, use it this way: "그때 같이 식사해요." Informal circumstances, use it with the verb ending -(으)ㅂ시다. In this case, formally you would say, "그때 같이 식사합시다."

★ 좋아요. "That sounds good."
Use this expression when consenting to a proposal.

Track 082

Yujin	Paul, happy birthday.
Paul	Thank you. Yujin, when is your birthday?
Yujin	My lunar calendar birthday is August 15th.
Paul	Your lunar calendar birthday is August 15th…then, your birthday is on Chuseok?
Yujin	Yes, that's right.
Paul	Oh, really?

유진   폴 씨, 생일 축하합니다.

폴   감사합니다.
     유진 씨는 생일이 언제예요?

유진   음력 8월 15일이에요.

폴   음력 8월 15일. 그럼, 추석이 생일이에요?

유진   네, 맞아요.

폴   아, 그래요?

New Vocabulary

음력 lunar calendar
추석 Chuseok
     (Korean Thanksgiving)

New Expressions

축하합니다. Congratulations!
생일 축하합니다.
Happy Birthday.

Conversation Tips

★ **생일 축하합니다. "Happy birthday."**
Use the expression 축하합니다 when congratulating someone on something. Put the reason for congratulations (a noun) first, then the phrase "축하합니다."

★ **음력 생일 "Lunar calendar birthday"**
Koreans traditionally used the lunar calendar, but from 1894 on, the Western solar-based calendar and the lunar calendar have both been used together. A lunar calendar date occurs about one month after its corresponding solar calendar date. Now because of Western influence, the solar calendar is officially used for scheduling; however, the lunar calendar is used for certain holidays such as the Lunar New Year, Chuseok (Korean Thanksgiving), and traditional service days, and many older people in Korea still follow the lunar calendar when celebrating their birthdays.

● 축하 [추카]

When a final consonant 'ㄱ, ㄷ, ㅈ' is followed by an initial consonant 'ㅎ' or vice versa, the 'ㄱ, ㄷ, ㅈ' are pronounced as aspirated [ㅋ, ㅌ, ㅊ] sounds.

(1) ㄱ → [ㅋ]　국화 [구콰], 어떻게 [어떠케]

(2) ㄷ → [ㅌ]　맏형 [마텽], 좋다 [조타]

(3) ㅈ → [ㅊ]　젖히다 [저치다], 넣지 [너치]

Additional Vocabulary

Track 084

① 지난달
last month

② 이번 달
this month

③ 다음 달
next month

! Be careful

* 작년 is pronounced as [장년].

작년 last year
올해 this year
내년 next year

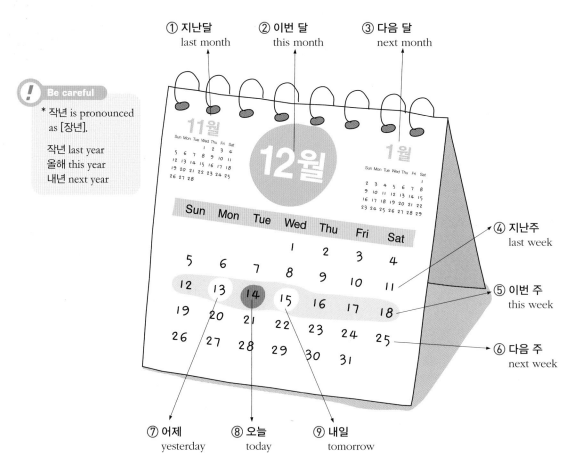

④ 지난주
last week

⑤ 이번 주
this week

⑥ 다음 주
next week

⑦ 어제
yesterday

⑧ 오늘
today

⑨ 내일
tomorrow

At a party

A Congratulations.
B Thank you.
When expressing congratulations.

A Please enjoy the meal.
B Thank you.
When inviting someone to share a meal.

※ When you have been invited to a meal, before starting to eat, say:
잘 먹겠습니다. "Thank you. (lit. I will eat it well.)"

A Please eat some more.
B No, I'm fine.
When inviting someone to eat more.

※ When you have been invited to a meal, after eating, say: 잘 먹었습니다. "Thank you. (lit. I ate it well.)"

Grammar

▶ Write the date as shown in the example below. (1~2)

며칠이에요?

Ex.

3월 25일 → <u>삼 월 이십오 일</u>

1   7월 14일 → _____   2   10월 3일 → _____

▶ Choose the correct answer to complete the conversation. (3~5)

3   A   생일이 (ⓐ 어디예요? / ⓑ 며칠이에요?)

    B   3월 31일이에요.

4   A   파티가 (ⓐ 언제예요? / ⓑ 어디예요?)

    B   다음 주 금요일이에요.

5   A   오늘이 (ⓐ 언제예요? / ⓑ 며칠이에요?)

    B   9월 4일이에요.

▶ Complete the conversation. (6~7)

6   A   언제 파티가 있어요?

    B   11월 15일_____ 파티가 있어요.

7   A   _____ 회의가 있어요?

    B   다음 주 월요일에 회의가 있어요.

Listening

▶ Listen and choose the correct answer. (8~9)

Track 086

8 파티가 언제예요?

ⓐ 7월 13일   ⓑ 7월 14일   ⓒ 8월 13일   ⓓ 8월 14일

9 파티가 무슨 요일이에요?

ⓐ 금요일   ⓑ 토요일   ⓒ 일요일   ⓓ 월요일

Reading

▶ Read and choose the correct answer. (10~11)

10월 8일이 리에 씨 생일이에요. 목요일이에요.
그런데 목요일에 시간이 없어요.
그래서 리에 씨가 10월 9일 금요일에 파티해요.

10 리에 씨 생일이 며칠이에요?

ⓐ 시 월 팔 일   ⓑ 시 월 구 일   ⓒ 십 월 팔 일   ⓓ 십 월 구 일

11 뭐가 맞아요?

ⓐ 리에 씨 생일이 금요일이에요.   ⓑ 리에 씨가 10월 8일에 파디해요.

ⓒ 리에 씨가 목요일에 시간이 있어요.   ⓓ 리에 씨 생일 파티가 금요일이에요.

Answers p.277

A Word on Culture

쌀	실	연필	돈	마이크	책
well being	longevity	diliggence	wealth	singer	scholar

Q Have you ever been to a typical Korean birthday party?

Different societies and cultures have different birthday traditions as well as different ideas about which birthdays are particularly meaningful. The Jewish have special Bar/Bat Mitzvah celebrations at 13, some Americans consider "Sweet 16" or 21 a special birthday, and Koreans have special birthdays at 1 year old and 60 years old. The first birthday in Korea (not counting the day a child was born) is called 돌잔치, and the 60th birthday is called 환갑.

In the past, when infant mortality rates were high, 돌잔치 became a celebration for a child who survived. Family members, relatives, and close friends gathered together to share food and celebrate the health of the child, as well as foretell the child's future. This foretelling is called 돌잡이. The child is seated before objects which are thought to symbolize his or her future, such as uncooked rice, a pencil, and a very long piece of string. The object that the child picks tells his or her fortune. So if he or she picks rice, Koreans believe the child will never have to worry about eating and therefore will live a comfortable, good life. A pencil or book means the child will become a scholar; string means the child will have a long life. More recently people have added money, lotto tickets, a microphone, and other everyday objects to the table to represent more contemporary professions and lifestyles.

환갑 also originates in the past when life expectancies were short and it was relatively rare to reach the age of 60; it celebrates a parent's longevity. Children throw 환갑 (sometimes called 회갑) for their parents, present them with new clothes, and invite all their relatives for the celebration.

Chapter 8 보통 아침 8시 30분에 회사에 가요.

- Expressing time
- The question words 몇 시 "what time" and 몇 시에 "what time"
- The marker for destination 에
- The markers ···부터 ···까지 "from ··· to ···"

● **Expressing time**

When reading time in Korean, hours and minutes are read differently. Hours are read using native Korean numbers, while minutes are read using Sino-Korean numbers.

When speaking, Korean people usually use the 12-hour time system, and the part of the day is given before the time.

아침 8시예요.	It's 8 o'clock in the morning.
저녁 8시예요.	It's 8 o'clock in the evening.

● **The question word 몇 시** "what time"

Appendix p.265

This question word 몇 시 is used when asking time.

1   A   지금 몇 시예요?   What time is it now?

    B   2 (두) 시예요.   It's 2:00.

2   A   지금 몇 시예요?   What time is it now?

    B   7 (일곱) 시 45 (사십오) 분이에요.   It's 7:45.

The marker for destination 에

With the verbs 가요/와요 (go/come), 에 is used after the name of the destination. Recall that we also learned to use the place marker 에 with 있어요/없어요 in Chapter 4.

A 어디에 가요?　　　　　　　　　Where are you going?

B 학교에 가요.　　　　　　　　　I'm going to school.

The question word 몇 시에 "what time"

When you want to ask what time something occurs, use the question word 몇 시 with the time marker 에.

A 몇 시에 집에 가요?　　　　　　What time do you go home?

B 저녁 8시에 집에 가요.　　　　　I go home at 8 in the evening.

The markers ⋯부터 ⋯까지 "from ⋯ to ⋯"

Appendix p.268

When discussing the duration of some event, use the marker 부터 to indicate the start time and the marker 까지 to indicate the ending time.

오후 3시부터 5시까지 회의가 있어요.　　I have a meeting from 3 to 5 in the afternoon.

When the context is clear, or when trying to emphasize one time or another, you can leave out either of them.

A 언제부터 휴가예요?　　　　　　When does your break start?

B 내일부터 휴가예요.　　　　　　It starts tomorrow.

Track **087**

Jane	Inho, where are you going now?
Inho	I'm going to work.
Jane	It is 7 o'clock now. Do you go to work early every day?
Inho	No, I have work to do this morning.
Jane	Really? What time do you usually go to work?
Inho	I usually go to work at 8:30 in the morning.
Jane	Then, at what time do you usually come back home?
Inho	I usually come back home at 7:30 in the evening.

제인	인호 씨, 지금 어디에 가요?
인호	회사에 가요.
제인	지금 7시예요. 매일 일찍 회사에 가요?
인호	아니요, 오늘 아침에 일이 있어요.
제인	그래요? 보통 몇 시에 회사에 가요?
인호	보통 아침 8시 30분에 회사에 가요.
제인	그럼, 보통 몇 시에 집에 와요?
인호	보통 저녁 7시 반에 집에 와요.

Conversation Tips

★ **The marker with 가요/와요 "go/come"**

The marker 에 is added to the destination which comes before the verbs 가요 (go) and 와요 (come). If the verb 와요 is used with the point of departure, it is written with the marker 에서 (from).

폴 씨가 저녁 7시에 집에 가요.	Paul is going home at 7.
선생님이 우리 집에 와요.	The teacher is coming to my home.
마크 씨가 미국에서 왔어요.	Mark came from America.

In Korean, use 가요 because Paul is leaving his present location and going to Mark's.

★ **몇 시에 vs. 언제**

You can also use 언제 instead of 몇 시에 in this expression. But don't use the time marker 에 with 언제.

몇 시에 집에 와요?
= 언제 (o) 언제에 (x)

New Vocabulary

지금 now
에 marker indicating the destination
가요 (I) go
시 hour (time)
매일 every day
일찍 early
오늘 today
보통 usually
몇 시에 what time
아침 morning
에 the marker for destination
일 work
분 minute
와요 (I) come
저녁 evening
반 half hour

New Expressions

지금 어디에 가요?
Where are you going now?

오늘 아침에 일이 있어요.
I have work to do this morning.

보통 몇 시에 회사에 가요?
What time do you usually go to the office?

몇 시에 집에 와요?
What time do you come home?

Track 088

몇 시에
집에 와요?

Rie	Paul, where are you going now?
Paul	I'm going to school.
Rie	From what time to what time are you usually in class?
Paul	I'm usually in class from 9 in the morning to 1 in the afternoon.
Rie	Then, what time do you come home?
Paul	I come home around 3 PM.

리에 폴 씨, 지금 어디에 가요?

폴 학교에 가요.

리에 보통 몇 시부터 몇 시까지 수업이 있어요?

폴 보통 아침 9시부터 오후 1시까지 수업이
있어요.

리에 그럼, 몇 시에 집에 와요?

폴 오후 3시쯤에 집에 와요.

New Vocabulary

학교 school
부터 from (time)
까지 to (time)
수업 class
오후 afternoon
쯤 around

New Expressions

학교에 가요.
I'm going to school.
몇 시부터 몇 시까지 수업이 있어요?
From what time to what time are you in class?
오후 3시쯤에 집에 와요.
I come home around 3 PM.

Conversation Tips

★ **From the largest to the smallest: time**
Just like with dates, times are read from the largest to the smallest unit:

금요일 아침 9시 (O)   9시 아침 금요일 (X)

★ **Order within a sentence: (time)에 + (place)에 + 와요**
In Korean, word order is quite free. So, it does not matter whether the time comes first or the place comes first as long as you write the verb 와요 at the end of the sentence.

저녁 7시에 집에 와요.   I come home at 7 in the evening.

★ **쯤 "about, around, almost, something like, or so"**
Used when roughly estimating numbers or time.

● 옷 [옫], 옷이 [오시]

In the first example, the final consonant '人' in 옷 is by rule pronounced as [ㄷ] when by itself (the next syllable is not followed by an ending with an initial vowel of the next syllable).

In the second example, when a word ending in a final consonant '人' is followed by a vowel (as in 옷이), the final consonant '人' is read as if it is the initial consonant of the next syllable.

(1) 낮 [낟], 낮이 [나지]

(2) 앞 [압], 앞에 [아페]

(3) 부엌 [부억], 부엌에 [부어케]

Additional Vocabulary

Track 090

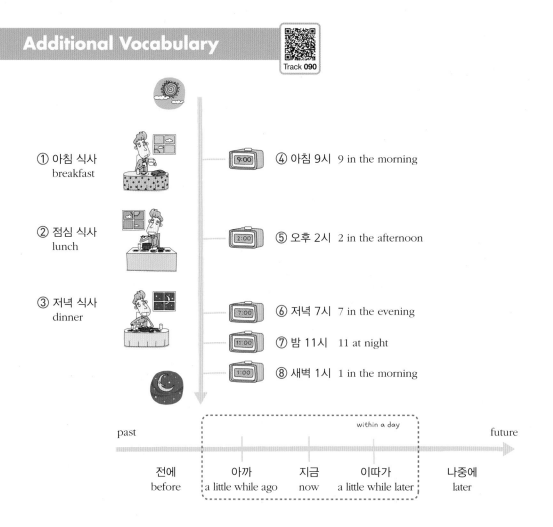

① 아침 식사
breakfast

② 점심 식사
lunch

③ 저녁 식사
dinner

④ 아침 9시 9 in the morning

⑤ 오후 2시 2 in the afternoon

⑥ 저녁 7시 7 in the evening

⑦ 밤 11시 11 at night

⑧ 새벽 1시 1 in the morning

within a day

past   future

전에   아까   지금   이따가   나중에
before   a little while ago   now   a little while later   later

In Korean, the same meaning may be said in different ways, depending on the situation and whom you are talking to.

Apologies

A I'm sorry.

B It's OK.

When speaking politely in a formal situation.
For instance, to a customer, a person who is older than you, or a stranger.

A I'm sorry.

B It's OK.

When speaking politely in a semi-formal situation.
For instance, to a close co-worker.

A I'm sorry.

B It's OK.

When speaking friendly in an informal situation.
For instance, to a classmate or a childhood friend.

Grammar

▶ Look at the picture and write the correct time. (1~2)

지금 몇 시예요?

Ex. → 다섯 시 십 분이에요.

1 → _____ .

2 → _____ .

▶ Look at the picture and complete the conversation. (3~4)

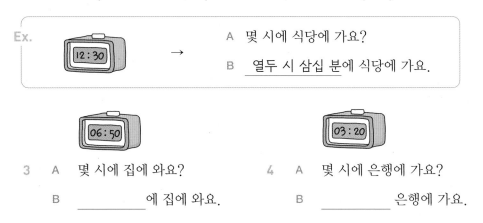

Ex. →
A 몇 시에 식당에 가요?
B 열두 시 삼십 분 에 식당에 가요.

3 A 몇 시에 집에 와요?

B _____에 집에 와요.

4 A 몇 시에 은행에 가요?

B _____은행에 가요.

▶ Look at the picture and complete the conversation. (5~6)

5 A 몇 시부터 몇 시까지 회의가 있어요?

B 1시_____ 2시 30분_____ 회의가 있어요.

START → FINISH

6 A 몇 시부터 몇 시까지 수업이 있어요?

B _____ 수업이 있어요.

START → FINISH

▶ Listen and indicate the time. (7~9)

7

8

9

▶ Listen and write the correct answer.

10 인호 씨가 어디에 가요?　　회사　→　(1) _____　→　집

몇 시에 가요?

(2) 　→　(3) 04 : 20 　→　(3)

Reading

▶ Read and complete the table.

11

Schedule	
TIME	TO DO
(1)	학교
10:00~1:00	(2)
(3)	회사
(4)	회의
7:00	(5)

아홉 시 삼십 분에 학교에 가요.

열 시부터 한 시까지 한국어 수업이 있어요.

그리고 두 시에 회사에 가요.

세 시 반부터 다섯 시까지 회의가 있어요.

일곱 시에 집에 가요.

Answers p.277

A Word on Culture

Q When meeting a Korean, what's the best way to greet him or her?

When you meet someone, greet him with "안녕하세요?" no matter the time of day. There is no equivalent to "good morning", "good afternoon", or "good evening", so you can always use "안녕하세요?"

But what if you see someone in the morning and then again later in the day? In that case, try this: ask "식사했어요?" (Have you eaten?) When Koreans run into each other around a mealtime, they often ask each other if they have eaten yet. But don't misunderstand-it is not an invitation to eat together, just a greeting.

In Korea, meals are common subjects when making small talk. When passing a friend on the street, you might ask whether that person has eaten yet, and suggest that next time you go out for a bite together. But do not take these proposals too seriously. They are just ways of greeting and making conversation, not serious invitations.

Be that as it may, when it comes time for a Korean to really invite you to a meal, you will find that Koreans are not stingy. Koreans believe that courtesy requires making sure that a guest will be presented with such an abundance of food that there is no possibility of running out. At the beginning of the meal, the host will say "많이 드세요." (lit. Please eat a lot.)

It is the guest's difficult duty to try to consume all the food, which has been painstakingly prepared by the host. So while it may not be the guest's intention, he often ends up overeating.

So, when you have a chance, give these greetings a try: "식사했어요?" and "많이 드세요."

Chapter 9 집에 지하철로 가요.

▫ Time duration

▫ The markers ···에서 ···까지 "from ··· to ···"

▫ The question words 어떻게 "how" and
얼마나 "how long / how much time"

▫ The marker (으)로: means of transportation

Time duration

Appendix p.268

To express time duration, the verb 걸려요 is used after the length of time. 분 (minutes), 일 (days), 년 (years) are expressed with the Sino-Korean numbers, and 시간 (hours), 달 (months) are expressed with the native Korean numbers.

(시간이)	10분 십	걸려요.	It takes	10 minutes.
	5시간 다섯			5 hours.
	3일 삼			3 days.

! Be careful

Don't mix up 시 and 시간 !

지금 1시예요. [time]
1시간 걸려요. [time duration]

<Exception>

| 1 day : 1일 (x) | 2 days : 2일 (x) |
| 하루 (o) | 이틀 (o) |

The markers ···에서 ···까지 "from ··· to ···"

Appendix p.268

To express distance, place the marker 에서 after the departure/starting place you've left from and 까지 after the arrival place. If the context is clear, one of these can disappear.

(집에서) 회사까지 50분 걸려요.

It takes 50 minutes (from the house) to the office.

? I wonder...

···부터 ···까지 [time]
···에서 ···까지 [space]

The question word 얼마나 "how long/how much time"

When asking about time duration, use the question word 얼마나. When the context is clear, you can drop the phrase 시간이.

A   여기에서 학교까지 (시간이) 얼마나 걸려요?
     How much time does it take from here to school?

B   1시간 10분 걸려요.   It takes 1 hour 10 minutes.
    한   십

The marker (으)로: means of transportation

When expressing the means by which you go somewhere, use the marker (으)로. If the means of transportation ends in a vowel, just use 로; if it ends in a consonant, use 으로.

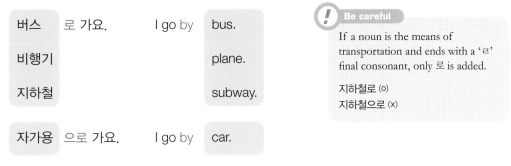

버스	로 가요.	I go by	bus.
비행기			plane.
지하철			subway.

| 자가용 | 으로 가요. | I go by | car. |

> **! Be careful**
>
> If a noun is the means of transportation and ends with a '르' final consonant, only 로 is added.
>
> 지하철로 (o)
> 지하철으로 (x)

※ 걸어서 가요. I go on foot.

The question word 어떻게 "how"

When asking someone how they will get somewhere, use the question word 어떻게.

1 A 어떻게 중국에 가요? How are you going to China?

   B 비행기로 가요. I'm going by plane.

2 A 부산에서 어떻게 서울에 와요? How are you coming to Seoul from Busan?

   B 기차로 와요. I'm coming by train.

Track 094

Satoru	Where is your house?
Yujin	It's in Mokdong.
Satoru	Is Mokdong far from here?
Yujin	No, it's close.
Satoru	From here, how long does it take to get to Mokdong?
Yujin	About 30 minutes.
Satoru	Are you going on foot?
Yujin	No, I am going by subway.

사토루   집이 어디예요?

유진   목동이에요.

사토루   목동이 여기에서 멀어요?

유진   아니요, 가까워요.

사토루   여기에서 목동까지 시간이 얼마나 걸려요?

유진   30분쯤 걸려요.

사토루   걸어서 가요?

유진   아니요, 지하철로 가요.

Conversation Tips

★ **The marker 에서 vs. The marker 부터**
In Korean, the marker 에서 expresses "from" for space while the marker 부터 expresses "from" for time.

(Space) [Starting point]에서 [destination]까지: 한국에서 미국까지 from Korea to USA
(Time) [Starting time]부터 [end time]까지: 3시부터 5시까지   from 3:00 to 5:00

★ **30분 vs. 반**
When speaking about duration, note that although "1시간 반 걸려요." is fine, you cannot say "반 걸려요."

30분 걸려요. (O)   1시간 30분 걸려요. (O)
= 반 (x)   = 1시간 반 (O)

New Vocabulary

목동 Mokdong (area of Seoul)
에서 from (place)
까지 to (place)
여기에서 from here
멀어요 (it is) far
가까워요 (it is) close
시간 hour (time duration)
얼마나 how long
걸려요 it takes (time)
걸어서 on foot
지하철 subway
(으)로 the marker for means of transportation

New Expressions

집이 어디예요?
Where is your house?

목동이 여기에서 멀어요?
Is Mokdong far from here?

여기에서 목동까지 시간이 얼마나 걸려요?
From here, how long does it take to get to Mokdong?

걸어서 가요?
Are you going on foot?

지하철로 가요.
I am going by subway.

Rie	At what time do you usually wake up?
James	I usually wake up at 6 in the morning.
Rie	Why do you wake up so early?
James	The school is really far from my house.
Rie	How much time does it take?
James	About 1 hour and 20 minutes.
Rie	Wow! That's really far. Then, how do you come to school?
James	I come by bus.

리에 　보통 몇 시에 일어나요?

제임스 보통 아침 6시에 일어나요.

리에 　왜 일찍 일어나요?

제임스 집에서 학교까지 너무 멀어요.

리에 　시간이 얼마나 걸려요?

제임스 1시간 20분쯤 걸려요.

리에 　와! 정말 멀어요.
　　　그럼, 어떻게 학교에 와요?

제임스 버스로 와요.

New Vocabulary

일어나요 (I) wake up
왜 why
너무 too (much)
시간 time
정말 really
어떻게 how
버스 bus

New Expressions

보통 몇 시에 일어나요?
What time do you usually wake up?

왜 일찍 일어나요?
What do you wake up so early?

너무 멀어요. It is too far away.

와! Wow!

정말 멀어요. That's really far.

어떻게 학교에 와요?
How do you come to school?

버스로 와요. I come by bus.

Conversation Tips

★ **나와요 "Come out"**
나와요 is a combination of two verbs (나다 + 오다).

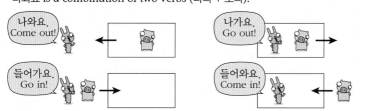

● 지하철로

The consonant '르' is pronounced differently depending upon its position. A final consonant '르' is pronounced more like the English [ℓ] sound. An initial consonant '르' is pronounced more like the English [r] sound (closer to Spanish tapped [r]). When a final consonant '르' is immediately followed by an initial consonant '르' both are pronounced as [ℓ].

(1) 걸려요

(2) 어울려요

(3) 불러요

Additional Vocabulary

Track 097

①

②

③

1 자동차(로)	(by) car
2 버스(로)	(by) bus
3 지하철(로)	(by) subway
4 택시(로)	(by) taxi
5 비행기(로)	(by) plane
6 기차(로)	(by) train
7 배(로)	(by) ship, boat
8 자전거(로)	(by) bicycle
9 걸어서	on foot

④

⑤

⑥

⑦

⑧

⑨

Common everyday expressions

A Please wait a minute.
B Take your time.

A I'm sorry.
B Don't worry about it.

A Are you OK?
B No problem.

A How long does it take?
B It depends.

Grammar

▶ Look at the picture and write the correct answer. (1~3)

시간이 얼마나 걸려요?

1　`01:00` ┄┄▶ `01:30`　＿＿＿＿＿＿＿＿ 걸려요.

2　`04:00` ┄┄▶ `05:00`　＿＿＿＿＿＿＿＿ 걸려요.

3　`06:00` ┄┄▶ `08:40`　＿＿＿＿＿＿＿＿ 걸려요.

▶ Look at the picture and complete the conversation. (4~6)

4　A 집에서 회사까지 어떻게 가요?

　　B (1) ＿＿＿＿＿＿＿ 가요.

　　A 시간이 얼마나 걸려요?

　　B (2) ＿＿＿＿＿＿＿ 걸려요.

집　　회사

8:15　　9:00

5　A 한국에서 일본까지 어떻게 가요?

　　B (1) ＿＿＿＿＿＿＿＿＿＿.

　　A 시간이 얼마나 걸려요?

　　B (2) ＿＿＿＿＿＿＿＿＿＿.

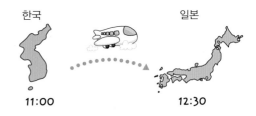

한국　　일본

11:00　　12:30

6　A 서울에서 부산까지 어떻게 가요?

　　B (1) ＿＿＿＿＿＿＿＿＿＿.

　　A 시간이 얼마나 걸려요?

　　B (2) ＿＿＿＿＿＿＿＿＿＿.

서울　　부산

2:30　　5:30

▶ Look at the picture. Listen and choose the correct answer. (7~9)

Track 099

7   ⓐ   ⓑ   ⓒ   ⓓ

8   ⓐ   ⓑ   ⓒ   ⓓ

9   ⓐ   ⓑ   ⓒ   ⓓ

08:00 ···▸ 08:40

집   학교

Reading

▶ Read and choose the correct answer. (10~11)

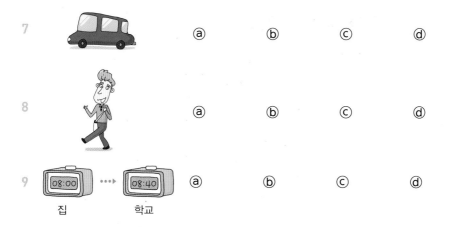

집에서 회사까지 멀어요. 시간이 많이 걸려요.
버스로 한 시간 십 분 걸려요. 지하철로 오십오 분 걸려요.
자동차로 사십 분 걸려요. 그런데 저는 자동차가 없어요.
그래서 보통 지하철로 회사에 가요.

제임스

10   집에서 회사까지 버스로 시간이 얼마나 걸려요?

    ⓐ 10일 걸려요.   ⓑ 1월 1일이에요.

    ⓒ 1시 10분이에요.   ⓓ 1시간 10분 걸려요.

11   뭐가 맞아요?

    ⓐ 55분에 집에 가요.   ⓑ 회사가 집에서 멀어요.

    ⓒ 보통 버스로 회사에 가요.   ⓓ 제임스 씨는 자동차가 있어요.

Answers p.278

A Word on Culture

Q Seoul's public transportation

Almost all foreigners living in Seoul agree that Seoul's transportation system is inexpensive. If you are living in the west part of Seoul, say near Gimpo airport, and want to go to North Seoul's Mt. Bukhan, it will only cost you 1,000-2,000 won (between one and two dollars). Is it because the area of Seoul is small? Rather, the reason Seoul's transportation system is so cheap and well-developed is because of its population – Seoul is home to at least 20% of South Korea's population, about 10 million people (2017 statistic). Need to hop on a bus or subway? Read on!

First, if you're thinking about staying in Seoul for more than a week, it's a good idea to buy a transportation card. Each time you ride a bus or subway, you simply put the transportation card against the card reader when getting on and off. Of course, you can also use cash, but there's no benefit over using a transportation card for transit passengers. When using a transportation card, if you get off one bus or subway and get on another within 30 minutes, you don't have to pay extra. If your journey is longer than 10km, you'll have to pay a mere 100 won more (about 10 cents). In addition, if you use a transportation card instead of cash, you get a 100 won discount for each trip.

In addition to being affordable, traveling by bus or subway is often faster than by car. While the roadways are jammed with traffic, subways run frequently and on time. Even the buses are often much faster than cars because, during peak traffic times, many roads have a special lane for buses only. You can use a transportation card to take taxis, borrow bicycles, and make purchases in 24-hour convenience stores.

For more information on Seoul's public transportation system, see the Seoul City site: http://english.seoul.go.kr/policy-information/traffic

Chapter 10 전부 얼마예요?

- Reading prices
- The question word 얼마 "how much"
- (noun) 주세요 "Give me (noun) please"
- The marker 하고 "and" (used only with nouns)

● Reading prices

In Korean, prices are read with Sino-Korean numbers. Although a comma is commonly placed after 3 digits, numbers are read with the basic unit 만 (10,000), the fourth digit.

원 Korean currency: won

Although in English we say "one thousand," "one hundred," etc., in Korean, a number starting with one, the "one" is not said.

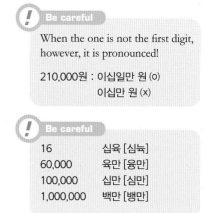

> **!** Be careful
>
> When the one is not the first digit, however, it is pronounced!
>
> 210,000원 : 이십일만 원 (o)
> 이십만 원 (x)

> **!** Be careful
>
> | 16 | 십육 [심뉵] |
> | 60,000 | 육만 [융만] |
> | 100,000 | 십만 [심만] |
> | 1,000,000 | 백만 [뱅만] |

● The question word 얼마 "how much"

Use the question word 얼마 in order to ask about price. 얼마 is followed by -예요, and 얼마예요 always goes at the end of the sentence.

A 커피가 얼마예요?   How much is this coffee?

B 3,500원이에요.   It is 3,500 won.

표 2장 주세요.
Give me two tickets.

네, 알겠습니다.
All right.

● (noun) 주세요 "Give me (noun) please"

Use this expression when asking for something. After the thing (noun) you're asking for, use 주세요. To make this even more polite, use 좀 (which also means "please") between the noun and 주세요.

1   A   영수증 주세요.   Give me a receipt please.

    B   여기 있어요.   Here it is.

2   A   물 좀 주세요.   Please give me some water.

    B   네, 알겠어요.   Yes, all right.

When asking for a specific amount of some noun, use the following formula:

noun	native Korean number	counting word		
커피	한	잔	주세요.	Give me one cup of coffee.
빵	두	개	주세요.	Give me two pieces of bread.
맥주	세	병	주세요.	Give me three bottles of beer.
표	네	장	주세요.	Give me four tickets.

● The marker 하고 "and" (used only with nouns)

To connect two nouns, use 하고 between them as you would use "and".

밥하고 김치   rice and kimchi

샌드위치하고 커피   sandwich and coffee

Track 100

clerk	Welcome. What would you like to order?
James	Give me one cafe latte and one piece of this bread.
clerk	OK.
James	How much is it all together?
clerk	It is 6,500 won.
	(After paying and the food is ready.)
clerk	Here it is. Goodbye.

직원   어서 오세요. 뭐 주문하시겠어요?

제임스   카페라테 하나하고 이 빵 하나 주세요.

직원   네, 알겠습니다.

제임스   전부 얼마예요?

직원   6,500원이에요.

(After paying and the food is ready.)

직원   여기 있습니다. 안녕히 가세요.

New Vocabulary

주문 order
카페라테 cafe latte
하나 one
빵 bread
(noun) 주세요 Give me (noun)
전부 all together, in total
얼마 how much
원 won (Korean currency)

New Expressions

어서 오세요. Welcome.
뭐 주문하시겠어요?
What would you like to order?
네, 알겠습니다. Yes, OK.
전부 얼마예요?
How much is it all together?
여기 있습니다. Here it is.
안녕히 가세요. Goodbye.
(used to someone who is leaving)

Conversation Tips

★ **Leaving out the counting word**

Often when ordering in a restaurant or coffee shop, people will leave out the counting word and use only the native Korean number to indicate the number of things being ordered. For example, when ordering in a restaurant, one might say, "비빔밥 하나 주세요."

★ **네, 알겠습니다. "Yes / OK / Will do / I understand."**

People in service industries will usually use formal speech in order to convey a polite atmosphere. You will hear the expression "네, 알겠습니다." in places such as airports, stores, cafes, and taxis to tell a customer that his / her request has been understood and will be followed. "알겠어요." is a bit less formal and used between people who know each other.

Track 101

Jane	Do you have train tickets to Busan for the morning of October 3rd?
clerk	I have KTX and Mugunghwa lines.
Jane	How much are they?
clerk	From Seoul to Busan, KTX is 45,000 won. Mugunghwa is 24,800 won.
Jane	How long does each one take?
clerk	KTX takes 2 hours and 30 minutes, and Mugunghwa takes 5 hours and 45 minutes.
Jane	Give me two KTX tickets.

제인   10월 3일 오전에 부산행 기차표 있어요?

직원   KTX하고 무궁화호가 있어요.

제인   얼마예요?

직원   서울에서 부산까지 KTX는 45,000원이에요.
무궁화호는 24,800원이에요.

제인   시간이 얼마나 걸려요?

직원   KTX는 2시간 30분, 무궁화호는 5시간 45분
걸려요.

제인   KTX 2장 주세요.

New Vocabulary

오전 morning [formal]

부산 Busan
(a large city in the south)

-행 indicating the arrival city

기차 train

표 ticket

KTX Korea Train Express
(super high-speed train)

무궁화호 Mugunghwa Express
(public passenger
train)

서울 Seoul
(South Korea's capital city)

장 counting word for tickets

New Expressions

부산행 기차표 있어요?
Do you have a train ticket to
Busan?

KTX 2장 주세요.
Give me two KTX tickets.

Conversation Tips

★ **부산행 기차표 "Train tickets going to Busan"**

In the phrase 부산행, 행 means "going in the direction of"- in this case, going in the direction of Busan. For the city of departure, the abbreviation 발 is used. 발 means "departing from".

뉴욕행 비행기 표   a plane ticket <u>going to</u> New York
서울발 기차표   a train ticket <u>departing from</u> Seoul

Track 102

전부 [전부] vs. 정부 [정부]

The '`ㄴ`' sound is pronounced, similar to an English [n], by the tongue touching behind the upper teeth. The final consonant '`ㅇ`' is produced, similar to the English [ng], from the throat. Practice differentiating these sounds in the following examples. Note that using the '`ㄴ`' or '`ㅇ`' changes the meaning of the word.

(1) 반 vs. 방

(2) 한 잔 vs. 한 장

(3) 불편해요 vs. 불평해요

Additional Vocabulary

Track 103

동전 coin

10원 (십 원)　　50원 (오십 원)　　100원 (백 원)　　500원 (오백 원)

지폐 bill

1,000원 (천 원)　　　　5,000원 (오천 원)

10,000원 (만 원)　　　　50,000원 (오만 원)

카드 Card

신용 카드　　　　　　현금 카드

In a restaurant

A   Will you eat this here? Will you take this to-go?
B   I'll take this to-go.
When ordering at a take-out cafe or restaurant.

※ When you will drink at the restaurant or cafe:
여기서 마실 거예요. "I'll drink it here." (for drinks)
여기서 먹을 거예요. "I'll eat it here." (for everything else)

A   Please heat this up for me.
B   OK, no problem.
When making requests to the cafe/restaurant staff.

A   Please give me some ice.
B   Sure, here you go.

Grammar

▸ Look at the picture and write the correct price. (1~2)

얼마예요?

Ex. ₩57,000 → <u>오만 칠천 원이에요.</u>

1 ₩9,500 → _____.

2 ₩103,000 → _____.

▸ Complete the conversation. (3~4)

3 A 모자가 _____예요?
  B 8,400원이에요.

4 A 핸드폰이 _____?
  B 275,000원이에요.

▸ Look at the picture and complete the conversation. (5~6)

5 A 커피가 (1) _____?
  B 6,700원이에요.
  A 커피 (2) _____ 잔 주세요.
  B 네, 알겠습니다.

6 A 빵이 (1) _____?
  B 3,200원이에요.
  A 빵 (2) _____.
  B 네, 알겠습니다.

▸ Listen and choose the correct answer. (7~8)

Track 105

7 커피가 얼마예요?

    ⓐ 5,600원   ⓑ 5,700원   ⓒ 6,600원   ⓓ 6,700원

8 우산이 얼마예요?

    ⓐ 37,500원   ⓑ 38,500원   ⓒ 47,500원   ⓓ 48,500원

▸ Listen and choose the correct answer.

Track 106

9   ⓐ 커피가 없어요.   ⓑ 녹차가 많이 있어요.

    ⓒ 커피가 4,500원이에요.   ⓓ 주스가 4,400원이에요.

Reading

▸ Read the ticket and mark O if correct or X if incorrect. (10~13)

10 이 표로 부산에 가요. ( )

11 시간이 2시간 10분 걸려요. ( )

12 팔 월 십 일에 가요. ( )

13 기차표가 오만 사천 원이에요. ( )

Answers p.278

A Word on Culture

감사합니다.

Q When eating with a Korean, how do you decide who pays?

If you have ever eaten out with a Korean, you know that Koreans are not accustomed to splitting the bill after a meal. Koreans look upon the practice of each paying separately for one's share as burdensome. Koreans know if they pay the bill this time, the other person will cover it next time. It's not that the next time has been planned in advance, but that if the opportunity presents itself, the other person will return the favor.

However, there are times when this unwritten rule does not hold true. When two people of unequal status (an older student and a younger student, a senior and junior co-worker, friends of different ages, for example) dine together, the older one usually pays for the younger one. Because people think that older people should treat younger people, the older one will not expect the favor to be returned the next time the pair dines together. The elder will have received the same good treatment from his own elders and is now returning the favor to the younger generation. So the younger or less senior person gets a free meal for the time being but knows he will treat someone younger or less senior than himself somewhere down the line.

In this culture, when good things happen you are also expected to treat. On one's birthday, upon getting a job or promotion, after getting married, or having a baby, one is expected to share one's happiness and good fortune with those around him or her. However, nowadays, people in the younger generation may choose to split the bill. How the bill is paid will differ by the situation, so watch what Koreans do.

This is Korea's give-and-take culture, how do you feel about taking part?

Chapter 11 어디에서 저녁 식사해요?

- 하다 verbs "to do"
- The place marker 에서
- Frequency
- The marker 하고 "with"

● 하다 verbs "to do"

Many nouns can be made into present tense verbs by adding the verb 해요.

noun			verb
일 + 해요	→		일해요
work			(I) work

Ex. 공부(study)해요, 운동(exercise)해요, 전화(call)해요, 요리(cook)해요, 운전(drive)해요

● The place marker 에서

Use the place marker 에서 to designate where an action takes place. This place marker 에서 is used with action verbs, with the exception of 있어요/없어요 and 가요/와요, which take the marker 에. When asking a question, use the question word 어디에서 with action verbs and 어디에 with 있어요/없어요 and 가요/와요.

1   A   어디에서 공부해요?   Where do you study?

    B   카페에서 공부해요.   I study at a café.

2   A   카페가 어디에 있어요?   Where is the café?

    B   카페가 지하철 역 앞에 있어요.   The café is located in front of the subway station.

3   A   어디에 가요?   Where are you going?

    B   약국에 가요.   I'm going to the pharmacy.

Frequency

Unlike in English, Koreans describe frequencies from the largest time unit to the smallest time unit. Use 에 (per) between the length of time and the frequency. Use the native Korean numbers for frequency.

하루에	2번 두	Twice	a day
일주일에	3번 세	Three times	a week
한 달에	2번 두	Twice	a month
일년에	1번 한	Once	a year

Use the question word 몇 번 "how many times" when asking about frequency.

A 일 년에 몇 번 여행 가요? How many times a year do you travel?

B 일 년에 2 (두) 번 여행 가요. I travel twice a year.

The marker 하고 "with"

When doing something with somebody, use 하고 after the person. Use 누구하고 when asking the question "with whom?"

A 누구하고 식사해요? Who are you eating with?

B 친구하고 같이 식사해요. I'm eating together with my friend.

C 저는 혼자 식사해요. I'm eating by myself.

Jane	What are you doing this afternoon?
Inho	I'm working.
Jane	What are you doing after that?
Inho	I'm having dinner.
Jane	Where are you having dinner?
Inho	I'm having dinner in a restaurant in the area near the office.
Jane	Who are you eating with?
Inho	I'm eating with my co-worker.

제인	오늘 오후에 뭐 해요?
인호	일해요.
제인	그다음에 뭐 해요?
인호	저녁 식사해요.
제인	어디에서 저녁 식사해요?
인호	회사 근처 식당에서 식사해요.
제인	누구하고 식사해요?
인호	회사 동료하고 식사해요.

New Vocabulary

하다 to do
일하다 to work
그다음에 after that
저녁 식사하다 to have dinner
에서 the place marker with action verbs
어디에서 where
식당 restaurant
식사하다 to have a meal
누구하고 with whom
동료 co-worker

New Expressions

오늘 오후에 뭐 해요?
What are you doing this afternoon?

그다음에 뭐 해요?
What are you doing after that?

어디에서 저녁 식사해요?
Where are you having dinner?

누구하고 식사해요?
Who are you eating with?

Conversation Tips

★ 뭐 해요? "What are you doing?"
The present tense can be used for explaining actions in the near future.

★ **From the largest unit to the smallest unit: time, place**
Unlike in English, Koreans generally describe locations from the largest unit to the smallest unit (for example, country, city, neighborhood).

회사 근처 식당에서 식사해요.
I'm eating at a restaurant in the area near the office.

Time is also ordered from the largest unit to the smallest.

오늘 저녁 7시에 뭐 해요? What are you doing at 7 this evening?

Track **108**

운동 자주 해요?

Jina	Paul, do you exercise often?
Paul	Yes, I exercise three times a week.
Jina	Where do you exercise?
Paul	In the park in front of my house. Jina, do you also exercise often?
Jina	No. I just go hiking in the mountains two or three times a year.
Paul	Oh, really?

지나 폴 씨, 운동 자주 해요?

폴 네, 일주일에 3번 해요.

지나 어디에서 해요?

폴 집 앞 공원에서 해요.
지나 씨도 운동 자주 해요?

지나 아니요. 저는 1년에 2–3번 등산만 해요.

폴 그래요?

New Vocabulary

운동하다 to exercise

자주 often, frequently

일주일 one week

에 per

번 counting word for time frequency

앞 front

공원 park

1년 one year

두세 번 two or three times

등산하다 to go hiking in the mountains

만 only, just
(The marker 만 placed after a noun designates uniqueness or exclusivity.)

Conversation Tips

★ **The location of adverbs**
Adverbs usually go in front of what they describe, so the adverb should go before the verb. With 해요 verbs, the adverb can go either before the noun or between the noun and 해요. The meaning is the same.

운동 자주 해요? = 자주 운동해요?

★ **세 번 vs. 삼 번**
"3번" is read as 세 번 using the native Korean number when you say the number of times and as 삼 번 using the Sino-Korean number when you read a number on a list.

Ex. 1년에 세 번 여행해요. I travel three times in a year.
삼 번 문제가 어려워요. The third question is difficult.

New Expressions

운동 자주 해요?
Do you exercise often?

일주일에 3 (세) 번 해요.
I do it three times a week.

1년에 2–3 (두세) 번 등산만 해요.
I just go hiking in the mountains two or three times a year.

● 동료 [동뇨]

When the final consonant '□, ○' are followed by the initial consonant 'ㄹ', the 'ㄹ' is pronounced as [ㄴ].

(1) ㄹ → [ㄴ] 정리 [정니]

(2) ㄹ → [ㄴ] 음력 [음녁]

(3) ㄹ → [ㄴ] 음료수 [음뇨수]

Additional Vocabulary

Track 110

① ② ③

④ ⑤ ⑥

⑦ ⑧ ⑨

1	일하다	to work
2	공부하다	to study
3	식사하다	to have a meal
4	전화하다	to call
5	운동하다	to exercise
6	얘기하다	to talk
7	운전하다	to drive
8	쇼핑하다	to shop
9	요리하다	to cook

	여행하다	to travel
	노래하다	to sing
	출발하다	to depart
	도착하다	to arrive
	준비하다	to prepare, get ready
	시작하다	to start
	연습하다	to practice
	회의하다	to have a meeting
	데이트하다	to go on a date
	이사하다	to move (to a new home)

Track 111

In Korean, use the same greeting "안녕하세요?" no matter the time of day. However, saying goodbye differs by the situation.

Saying goodbye

A See you tomorrow.
B See you tomorrow.
When leaving work or school.

A Have a good weekend.
B Paul, you have a good weekend too.
When leaving for the weekend.

A Have a good trip.
When saying farewell to someone leaving on a trip.

※ When saying farewell to someone leaving on a business trip:
출장 잘 다녀오세요. "Have a good business trip."

Quiz Yourself!

Grammar

▶ Look at the picture and choose the correct answer. (1~2)

뭐 해요?

1

ⓐ 식사해요

ⓑ 공부해요

2

ⓐ 운동해요

ⓑ 운전해요

▶ Choose the correct answer to complete the sentence. (3~5)

3   회사(에 / 에서) 가요. 회사(에 / 에서) 일해요.
     (1)   (2)

4   식당(에 / 에서) 가요. 식당(에 / 에서) 식사해요.
     (1)   (2)

5   집(에 / 에서) 와요. 집(에 / 에서) 자요.
    (1)   (2)

▶ Look at the picture and complete the conversation. (6~7)

6   A 누구하고 식사해요?

    B _____ 식사해요.

친구

7   A 누구하고 쇼핑해요?

    B _____ 쇼핑해요.

170 · Korean made easy for beginners (2nd edition)

▸ Look at the picture. Listen and choose the correct answer. (8~9)

Track 112

8 　　ⓐ　　　ⓑ　　9 　　ⓐ　　　ⓑ

　　　　　　　　　ⓒ　　　ⓓ　　　　　　　　　　　ⓒ　　　ⓓ

▸ Listen to the question and choose the correct answer.

Track 113

10　ⓐ 1시에 식사해요.　　　　　　ⓑ 토요일에 식사해요.

　　ⓒ 친구하고 식사해요.　　　　　ⓓ 일주일에 3번 식사해요.

Reading

▸ Read and mark O if correct or X if incorrect. (11~15)

아침 6시에 일어나요.
7시까지 집 옆 공원에서 운동해요.
그다음에 집에 가요. 샤워해요.
그리고 8시 10분에 집 앞 식당에서 아침 식사해요.
9시에 회사에 가요. 10시 30분부터 12시까지 회의해요.
그다음에 회사 옆 식당에서 동료하고 점심 식사해요.

11　집 앞 공원에서 운동해요.　　　　　(　　　)

12　아침 식사해요. 그 다음에 운동해요.　(　　　)

13　8시 10분에 식당에 있어요.　　　　(　　　)

14　회의 시간이 1시간 30분이에요.　　(　　　)

15　혼자 점심 식사해요.　　　　　　　(　　　)

Answers p.279

A Word on Culture

Q Do you know how to indicate respect using your hands?

You may have noticed that body language differs according to culture. For instance, in Korea, when greeting someone with "안녕하세요?", people bow their heads a bit to indicate respect. But did you know there are also ways in which you may indicate respect using your hands?

When giving or taking something from a stranger, someone older, someone of higher status, or someone with whom you have a formal relationship (such as a co-worker) use not one hand but two. If it is difficult to use both hands, you can take the object with your right hand as your left hand holds your right forearm. Koreans also shake hands like this–with the left arm holding on to the right forearm. Watch closely next time you see two Koreans meet, as they bow their heads slightly and shake hands this way.

Drinking is a common cultural activity (especially among men) with its own rich body language. When pouring for someone or having a drink poured for you, you should always hold the glass or bottle with two hands, arms extended. In the old days, the sleeves of traditional men's Korean clothing were very long so one had to extend one's arms out to receive a glass. Also, when drinking in front of a superior, turn your head a bit so that you are not facing him when you take a sip. This is another way of showing respect.

Koreans have become accustomed to this culture of paying respect to others through these various actions and postures; how do you feel about acquainting yourself with these?

Chapter 12 매주 일요일에 영화를 봐요.

- The informal polite form -아/어요 in the present tense
- The object marker 을/를
- Making suggestions "let's"
- (noun)은/는 어때요? "how about (noun)?"

한국 음식을 좋아해요?
Do you like Korean food?

네, 정말 **좋아해요**.
Yes, I really like it.

● **The Informal polite form -아/어요 in the present tense**

Appendix p.265

The infinitive form becomes the informal polite form by adding the ending -아/어요 to the verb stem. "Informal" refers to the type of situation; this form, for instance, is most widely used in daily life when shopping, buying tickets, and asking for directions. Conversely, the formal polite form -(스)ㅂ니다 which you will learn later, is used in business meetings, speeches, presentations, etc. (refer to page 245 for details).

Use the chart below to form all present tense verbs. The ending of the verb in the present tense depends on the verb stem.

> **?** I wonder...
>
> The infinitive form
>
> 보|다
> 먹|다
> verb stem

1. The verb 하다 becomes 해요.

    공부하다 (to study) → 공부해요 (study/studies)

2. If the verb stems has a '아' or '오' vowel, add -아요 to the stem to form the present tense.

살다	→	살 + -아요	→	살아요
자다	→	자 + -아요	→	자요
보다	→	보 + -아요	→	봐요

3. Add -어요 to all other verb stems to form the present tense.

먹다	→	먹 + -어요	→	먹어요
주다	→	주 + -어요	→	줘요
마시다	→	마시 + -어요	→	마셔요

    * Refer to page 265 for rules of combining certain verb stems with their corresponding verb ending form.

같이 커피를 마셔요. 🥤
Let's drink coffee together.

좋아요.
Sounds good.

The object marker 을/를

In Korean, objects are designated by the object marker 을/를. Objects and their 을/를 marker usually appear in front of the verb. In colloquial conversations, people often leave the object marker 을/를 out.

ending in a vowel	ending in a consonant
폴 씨가 친구를 만나요.	지나 씨가 음식을 먹어요.
Paul meets a friend.	Jina eats food.

Making suggestions "let's"

When making a suggestion "let's" use the present tense form -아/어요 as you normally would. You can also use the phrase 같이 "together" in front of the sentence.

A 같이 영화 봐요.　　　　　　Let's see a movie together.

B 좋아요.　　　　　　　　　Sounds good.

(noun)은/는 어때요? "how about (noun)?"

Use this expression to give a suggestion. Use the topic marker 은/는 after the noun and then ask 어때요?

A 금요일에 시간 있어요?　　　Do you have time on Friday?

B 아니요, 없어요.　　　　　　No, I don't.

A 그럼, 토요일은 어때요?　　　Then how about Saturday?

B 좋아요.　　　　　　　　　Sounds good.

Track **114**

Jina	Do you like Korean movies?
Paul	Yes, I really like them. How about you, Jina?
Jina	I like Korean movies, too. When do you usually go see a movie?
Paul	I see a movie every Sunday.
Jina	Oh, really? I also watch a movie every Sunday.
Paul	Then, let's see a movie together later.
Jina	OK

지나 한국 영화 좋아해요?

폴 네, 정말 좋아해요. 지나 씨는 어때요?

지나 저도 한국 영화를 좋아해요.
보통 언제 영화를 봐요?

폴 매주 일요일에 영화를 봐요.

지나 그래요? 저도 일요일마다 영화를 봐요.

폴 그럼, 나중에 같이 영화 봐요.

지나 그래요.

New Vocabulary

영화 movie, film
좋아하다 to like
(은/는) 어때요? How about …?
저도 me too
을/를 the object marker
보다 to see
매주 every week
일요일 Sunday
마다 each, every
나중에 later

New Expressions

지나 씨는 어때요?
How about you, Jina?

저도 …을/를 좋아해요.
I too… enjoy,

보통 언제 영화를 봐요?
When do you usually go see a movie?

매주 일요일에 (= 일요일마다)
every Sunday

나중에 같이 영화를 봐요.
Let's see a movie together later.

그래요. OK.

Conversation Tips

★ 저는 vs. 저도

Use the marker 은/는 to emphasize 저 (I) or draw attention to difference between yourself and someone else. On the other hand, using the marker 도 after 저 emphasizes similarity.

A 저는 운동을 좋아해요. 폴 씨는 어때요?
I like to exercise. How about you, Paul?

B 저도 운동을 좋아해요. I also like to exercise.

C 저는 운동을 안 좋아해요. I don't like to exercise.

Think about how you might emphasize "I" with your voice in English. The marker 은/는 has a similar function.

Track 115

Jane	Do you like Korean food?
Satoru	Yes, I like it. How about you, Jane?
Jane	I also like Korean food.
	So these days I'm learning how to cook Korean food.
Satoru	Oh, really? Who are you learning it from?
Jane	I'm learning from my friend.
Satoru	Is it fun?
Jane	Yes, let's make some together later.
Satoru	Sounds good.

제인 한국 음식 좋아해요?

사토루 네, 좋아해요. 제인 씨는 어때요?

제인 저도 한국 음식을 좋아해요.
그래서 요즘 한국 요리를 배워요.

사토루 그래요? 누구한테서 배워요?

제인 친구한테서 배워요.

사토루 재미있어요?

제인 네, 나중에 한번 같이 만들어요.

사토루 좋아요.

New Vocabulary

음식 food
그래서 so, therefore
요즘 these days
요리 cooking
배우다 to learn
한테서 from
누구한테서 from whom
친구 friend
재미있다 to be interesting, fun
한번 once
만들다 to make

New Expressions

누구한테서 배워요?
Who are you learning it from?

재미있어요? Is it interesting?

나중에 한번 같이 만들어요.
Let's make some together later.

좋아요. Sounds good.

Conversation Tips

★ 좋아해요 vs. 좋아요

좋아하다 is the verb for "to like," while 좋아요 takes on the form of an adjective, meaning "It's good./Sounds good." 좋아해요 takes the object marker 을/를. On the other hand, 좋아요 takes the subject marker 이/가. Be careful! These expressions look similar but the meaning is different!

마크 씨가 한국 음식을 좋아해요.　　Mark likes Korean food.
날씨가 좋아요.　　　　　　　　　The weather is good.

Track 116

읽어요 [일거요]

When a double final consonant is followed by a vowel (as in 읽어요), the second final consonant is pronounced as if it is the initial consonant of the next syllable.

(1) 밝아요 [발가요]

(2) 넓어요 [널버요]

(3) 앉아요 [안자요]

Additional Vocabulary

Track 117

① ② ③

④ ⑤ ⑥

⑦ ⑧ ⑨

1 일어나다	to get up
2 커피를 마시다	to drink coffee
3 책을 읽다	to read a book
4 음식을 먹다	to eat food
5 친구를 만나다	to meet friend(s)
6 책을 사다	to buy a book
7 영화를 보다	to watch a movie
8 음악을 듣다	to listen to music
9 자다	to sleep

말하다	to speak
놀다	to play
쉬다	to rest
만들다	to make
도와주다	to help
빌리다	to borrow
살다	to live
끝나다	to finish
쓰다	to write

Shopping

A Welcome. What are you looking for?

B Could you show me some t-shirts?

A How about this one?

B Do you have something different?

※ When asking for a different size:

큰 건 없어요? "Do you have something bigger?"

작은 건 없어요? "Do you have something smaller?"

(To soften a question, use "없어요?" instead of "있어요?")

A Can I try it on?

B Sure, go this way.

A Please give me this one.

※ When pointing to some clothes not near you:

저걸로 주세요. "Please give me that one."

※ When bargaining prices:

좀 깎아 주세요. "Please lower the price."

※ When leaving a store without making a purchase:

좀 더 보고 올게요. "I'll look around a bit and come back."

Grammar

▶ Look at the picture and choose the correct answer. (1~4)

1
ⓐ 자요
ⓑ 일어나요

2
ⓐ 마셔요
ⓑ 먹어요

3
ⓐ 읽어요
ⓑ 들어요

4
ⓐ 써요
ⓑ 만나요

▶ Complete the paragraph using -아/어요 in the present tense. (5~6)

5 마크 씨가 한국 회사에서 <u>일해요</u>. (일하다) 보통 저녁 6시에 일이 (1)_____. (끝
나다) 그리고 집에서 밥을 (2)_____. (먹다) 영화를 (3)_____. (보다) 보통
밤 11시에 (4)_____. (자다)

6 제인 씨가 영어 선생님이에요. 학원에서 영어를 (1)_____. (가르치다) 영어 학원이
강남에 (2)_____. (있다) 보통 수업 후에 친구를 (3)_____. (만나다) 친구하
고 커피를 (4)_____. (마시다)

▶ Choose the correct answer. (7~10)

7 A 폴 씨가 뭐 먹어요?
   B 점심(을 / 를) 먹어요.

8 A 마크 씨가 뭐 마셔요?
   B 커피(을 / 를) 마셔요.

9 A 제인 씨가 뭐 들어요?
   B 음악(을 / 를) 들어요.

10 A 리에 씨가 뭐 배워요?
    B 한국어(을 / 를) 배워요.

▶ Listen and fill in the correct numbers according to the sequence of Paul's actions.

Track 119

11

(   )   (1   )   (   )   (   )

Reading

▶ Read and correct three phrases based on the picture.

12

13 월	**14** 화	**15** 수	**16** 목	**17** 금	**18** 토	**19** 일
오후 1시 친구, 식사	아르바이트, 중국어 수업	집, 약속 ✕	운동, 공부	광주 여행, 기차	집	

월요일 <u>2시에</u> 친구하고 <u>영화를 봐요.</u>
     ⓐ → 1시에   ⓑ

화요일에 <u>아르바이트</u>가 있어요. <u>영어</u>를 가르쳐요.
      ⓒ   ⓓ

수요일에 집에 <u>있어요.</u> 목요일에 <u>운동해요.</u> 그리고 공부해요.
      ⓔ   ⓕ

금요일에 <u>경주</u>에 여행 가요. <u>기차로</u> 가요. <u>토요일에</u> 집에 와요.
      ⓖ   ⓗ   ⓘ

Answers p.278 and p.279

A Word on Culture

Q The "Korean wave"

The Korean cultural boom which started in the late 1990s began to exert a strong influence in Japan, China, and Southeast Asia around the time of the 2002 World Cup in the name of "Hallyu" or the "Korean Wave". Through the 2010s, the 'Korean Wave' garnered a following among people residing in Asia, United States, Europe, and South America. In the present, the 'Korean Wave' is not limited to popular cultures such as movies, dramas, and songs. Korean electronic products such as TVs, mobile phones, and automobiles, as well as Korean cosmetic products and fashion, and Korean foods which range from natural vegetarianism to intense flavors have gained immense popularity.

Among them, popular cultures including Korean movies, dramas, and songs are at the epicenter of the 'Korean Wave'. A variety of works and artists are loved for their uniqueness, thereby forming a diverse fan-base internationally. In the 2020s, K-pop groups like BTS have formed a global fandom and are receiving ecstatic support, and Korean films which received favorable reviews domestically have also received praise and recognition at international film festivals. Korean dramas are loved for everyday people and rank highly on Netflix's charts.

I would like to recommend that people who want to learn vivid Korean expressions and descriptions experience movies, dramas, and movies that provide a glimpse of Korean culture. You can get a glimpse of not only the Korean language which is used in everyday life but also the present Korean way of thinking and living.

Chapter 13

머리가 아파요.

- The descriptive use of the adjectives -아/어요 in the present tense
- Negating with 안
- The marker 도 "also"

추워요?
Are you cold?

아니요, **안** 추워요.
No, I'm not cold.

The descriptive use of the adjectives -아/어요 in the present tense *Appendix p.269*

In Korean, as in English, adjectives modify nouns. However, unlike English, adjectives in Korean have the function of describing the state of the subject in a sentence. In other words, adjectives can take on a descriptive use, in addition to the function of modifying nouns. The descriptive usage of Korean adjectives can be understood as an adjective in English used together with the verb to express the state of the sentence's subject (to be happy, to be sad, to be expensive, etc.) Korean adjectives do not require the verb 'be'. Instead, the adjective itself is used in conjunction with the ending of a verb to express the state of the subject of the sentence. Note that when a Korean adjective describes a state, it is always used with the subject marker 이/가.

좋다 (to be good)
날씨가 좋아요. The weather is good.

비싸다 (to be expensive)
옷이 비싸요. Clothing is expensive.

> **! Be careful**
>
> The verb 필요하다 ("to need") seems like it should take an object, but in Korean, this is a descriptive verb. You may find it helpful to think of this verb as "to be needed."
>
> 저는 연습이 필요해요. Practice is needed.

Negating with 안

안 is placed in front of verbs or adjectives to indicate negation. In the case of 하다 verbs, 안 is placed between the noun and 하다.

Descriptive verbs and action verbs, except 하다 action verbs.

안 자요.　　　　I don't sleep.
안 비싸요.　　　It is not expensive.
안 중요해요.　　It is not important.

> **! Be careful**
>
> 운동하다 (verb) "to exercise"
> → 운동 안 해요. I do not exercise.
> 피곤하다 (adjective) "to be tired"
> → 안 피곤해요. I am not tired.
>
> **An exception!**
> 좋아하다 (verb) "to like"
> → 생선 안 좋아해요. I do not like fish.

Remember, in the case of 하다 action verbs, the negation is placed before 하다.

일 안 해요.　　　I don't work.

The marker 도 "also"

If two sentences connected by 그리고 "and" are of the same structure, you can use the marker 도 "also, too" in the second sentence to emphasize commonality.

1. When using the marker 도, don't use the subject marker 이/가 or the object marker 을/를. The maker 도 replaces the subject maker 이/가 and the object marker 을/를.

> 비가 와요. 그리고 바람도 불어요.
> It's raining. And it's also windy.

> 아침을 먹어요. 그리고 커피도 마셔요.
> I eat breakfast. And I also drink coffee.

2. The maker 도 goes after the other markers, such as the markers 에 and 에서.

> 식당에 가요. 그리고 카페에도 가요.
> I go to the restaurant. And I also go to the café .

> 학교에서 공부해요. 그리고 집에서도 공부해요.
> I study at school. And I also study at home.

> 하고 "and" is used to connect two nouns,
> but 그리고 "and" is used to connect two sentences.
>
> 마크하고 폴 Mark <u>and</u> Paul
> 음식이 싸요. <u>그리고</u> 사람도 친절해요.
> The food is cheap. <u>And</u> the people are also friendly.

Track **120**

Yujin	Paul, are you sick?
Paul	No, I'm not sick. I'm just a bit tired.
Yujin	Why?
Paul	I have a lot of work these days. So I'm a bit tired.
Yujin	Be careful with your health.
Paul	I will. Thanks for your concern.

유진   폴 씨, 어디 아파요?

폴   아니요, 안 아파요. 그냥 좀 피곤해요.

유진   왜요?

폴   요즘 일이 너무 많아요.
        그래서 좀 피곤해요.

유진   건강 조심하세요.

폴   네, 고마워요.

New Vocabulary

아프다 to hurt
안 negation of verb
그냥 just
좀 a little, a bit
피곤하다 to be tired
많다 to be a lot
건강 health
조심하다 to be careful

New Expressions

어디 아파요? Are you sick?
그냥 좀 피곤해요.
I'm just a bit tired.
왜요? Why?
일이 너무 많아요.
I have a lot of work.
건강 조심하세요.
Be careful with your health.

Conversation Tips

★ 어디 아파요? "Are you sick?"
"어디 아파요?" means "Are you sick?" and does not necessarily mean "Where does it hurt?" you can normally figure out which meaning it is based on context.

★ 좀 피곤해요. "I'm a bit tired."
좀 is a short form of 조금. Although this looks the same as "please," the meaning is different.

Track **121**

Rie	James, did you catch a cold?
James	Yes.
Rie	Is it serious?
James	Yes, I have a little headache. And I also have a cough.
Rie	Oh, really? The weather is cold these days. So be careful.
James	OK. I will.

리에　제임스 씨, 감기에 걸렸어요?

제임스　네.

리에　많이 아파요?

제임스　네, 머리가 좀 아파요.
　　　그리고 기침도 나요.

리에　그래요? 요즘 날씨가 추워요.
　　　그러니까 조심하세요.

제임스　네, 그럴게요.

New Vocabulary

감기 a cold
감기에 걸리다 to catch a cold
많이 a lot
머리 head
그리고 and (used between sentences)
기침 cough
기침이 나다 to have a cough
날씨 weather
춥다 to be cold
그러니까 so, therefore

New Expressions

감기에 걸렸어요?
Did you catch a cold?

많이 아파요? Is it serious?

머리가 좀 아파요.
I have a little headache.

기침도 나요. I also cough.

요즘 날씨가 추워요.
The weather is cold these days.

그럴게요. I will.

Conversation Tips

★ **그래서 vs. 그러니까**

그래서 and 그러니까 can mean "so" when it is placed between two sentences (the reason - the result), so 그래서 and 그러니까 may often be used interchangeably.

한국에서 일해요. 그래서 한국어를 배워요. I work in Korea. So, I learn Korean.
　　　= 그러니까 (0)

However, do not use 그래서 before a command or suggestion. Instead, use 그러니까.

날씨가 추워요. 그러니까 조심하세요.　　The weather is cold. So, be careful.
　　　= 그래서 (x)

Pronunciation

Track 122

● 많아요 [마나요] / 만나요 [만나요]

The following words have different meanings but similar pronunciations.

(1) 좋아요 (It's good) / 추워요 (It's cold)

(2) 쉬워요 (It's easy) / 쉬어요 (Take a rest)

(3) 조용해요 (It's quiet) / 중요해요 (It's important)

Additional Vocabulary

Track 123

① 귀 ears
② 코 nose
③ 어깨 shoulders
④ 배 belly
⑤ 손 hand
⑥ 손가락 finger
⑩ 머리 head
⑨ 눈 eye
⑧ 입 mouth
⑦ 가슴 chest
⑲ 머리(카락) hair
⑪ 이 teeth
⑫ 팔 arms
⑱ 목 neck
⑰ 허리 waist, lower back
⑬ 무릎 knee
⑭ 발 foot
⑯ 다리 legs
⑮ 발가락 toe

Caring for others

A   How are you feeling today?
B   Good.
When asking about someone's mood.

※ When you're not feeling great:
   별로예요. "Not very good."

A   Are you sick?
B   I have a little headache.
When someone looks different than usual.

※ When someone is not sick but has a strange or
   uncomfortable expression:
   무슨 일 있어요? "Is something the matter?"

A   It's been a long time.
B   It's been a long time.
When meeting someone you haven't seen in a long
time.

A   How are you doing these days?
B   I'm doing well.
When asking someone how he/she has been.

Other expressions
A   그동안 어떻게 지냈어요? "How have you been doing?"
B   잘 지냈어요. "I've been doing fine."

Grammar

▶ Look at the picture and choose the correct answer. (1~4)

1 기분이 ⓐ 좋아요.

ⓑ 나빠요.

2 책이 ⓐ 싸요.

ⓑ 비싸요.

3 영화가 ⓐ 재미있어요.

ⓑ 재미없어요.

4 날씨가 ⓐ 추워요.

ⓑ 더워요.

▶ Complete the conversation as shown in the example below. (5~7)

Ex. A 추워요?

B 아니요, <u>안 추워요</u>.

5 A 바빠요?

B 아니요, _____.

6 A 피곤해요?

B 아니요, _____.

7 A 운동해요?

B 아니요, _____.

▶ Choose the correct answer and complete the sentence. (8~10)

그리고	그런데	그래서

8 머리가 아파요. _____ 약을 먹어요.

9 한국어 공부가 재미있어요. _____ 어려워요.

10 영어 말하기가 쉬워요. _____ 듣기도 쉬워요.

Listening

▶ Listen and mark what Jane did.

Track **125**

11
(일해요)	운동해요	핸드폰을 봐요	친구를 만나요
전화해요	공부해요	책을 읽어요	음악을 들어요

▶ Listen and choose the correct answer to complete the sentence.

Track **126**

12 민수 씨가 일이 많아요. 그래서 _____.

ⓐ   ⓑ   ⓒ   ⓓ

Reading

▶ Read and match the picture with the condition. (13~15)

13
열이 나요. 기침도 나요.
그리고 추워요.
그래서 오늘은 일 안 해요.

•

 • ⓐ 아파요

14
요즘 너무 바빠요.
회의가 많이 있어요.
오늘도 집에 10시에 가요.

•

 • ⓑ  기분이 좋아요.

15
저는 여행을 좋아해요.
오늘 제주도에 여행 가요.
지금 비행기로 가요.

•

 • ⓒ  피곤해요.

Answers p.279

A Word on Culture

Q Why is it that Koreans say "괜찮아요" so much?

During the course of a day in Korea, you will probably hear the phrase "괜찮아요" many times. Whether you are asking about the weather or someone's mood, the typical response will probably be "괜찮아요." Korean culture associates strong negatives with bad manners. Rather than speaking clearly and frankly about thoughts and feelings, etiquette requires responses like "괜찮아요" (OK) or "별로예요" (not particularly good).

The expression "괜찮아요" thus occurs in many kinds of situations, with many different meanings. "괜찮아요" is used not only as a polite substitute for when one's mood is bad but it is also used to accept thanks and apologies. When someone is pressing you to eat more, use "괜찮아요" as a polite refusal like "No, thanks." Koreans ask "괜찮아요?" to find out if a sick friend is getting better, reassure someone who has made a mistake with "괜찮아요" and ask a sad friend "괜찮아요?"

The many varied uses of "괜찮아요" can cause confusion for someone just learning to speak Korean. When trying to understand this phrase, pay careful attention to the speaker's expression, voice, and body language to understand his or her meaning. If you find yourself getting frustrated, tip your head back and shout, "괜찮아요" to give this phrase a try!

Chapter 14

지난주에 제주도에 여행 갔어요.

- The informal polite form of the verbs and adjectives -았/었어요 in the past tense
- The word for time duration 동안
- The superlative 제일 "the most"
- Comparisons using 보다 더 "more than"

얼마 동안 한국에서 살았어요?
How long have you lived in Korea?

2년 동안 **살았어요.**
I've lived in Korea for two years.

● **The informal polite form of the verbs and adjectives -았/었어요 in the past tense**

In the case of verbs or adjectives in the past tense, use the -았/었어요 stem ending. If the stem ends in 하, change it to 했어요. When the end of the syllable of a stem ends with vowels 'ㅏ' or 'ㅗ', -았어요 is used. In all other cases, -었어요 is used.

present			past
운동하다	운동하 + -었어요	→	운동했어요
좋다	좋 + -았어요	→	좋았어요
먹다	먹 + -었어요	→	먹었어요

어제 공원에서 운동했어요.   I exercised at the park yesterday.

지난주에 조금 바빴어요.   I was a little busy last week.

● **The word for time duration 동안**

Use the word 동안 after a length of time to designate duration. When asking a question about a length of time, use the question word 얼마 followed by 동안.

1   A   얼마 동안 부산에서 일했어요?   How long did you work in Busan?

    B   6 (여섯) 달 동안 **일했어요.**   I worked there for 6 months.

2   A   얼마 동안 서울에서 살았어요?   How long did you live in Seoul?

    B   4 (사) 년 동안 **살았어요.**   I lived there for 4 years.

 I wonder...

There are two ways to express duration in months.

two months: 2 (두) 달 (달 takes the native Korean number.)
           2 (이) 개월 (개월 takes the Sino-Korean number.)

The superlative 제일 "the most"

When you want to say something is the most or the best, use 제일 before the adjectives, adverbs, and verbs whether it is a question or an answer.

A 무슨 영화가 제일 재미있어요?　What kind of movies do you find the most interesting?

B 코미디 영화가 제일 재미있어요.　Comedies are the most interesting.

> **! Be careful**
>
> Do not use 제일 before a noun.
>
> best friend:
> 제일 친구 (x)
> 제일 좋은 친구 (o)

Comparisons using 보다 더 "more than"

When comparing two things, use the marker 보다 after the thing of comparison and 더 before the adjectives, adverbs, and the verbs to mean "more".

여름이 겨울보다 더 좋아요.　Summer is better than winter.

Use 중에서 when asking someone to make a choice among a group of things.

A 빨간색하고 파란색 중에서 뭐가 더 좋아요?
Between red and blue which is better?

B 빨간색이 파란색보다 더 좋아요.
Red is better than blue.

더 "more"
　이게 더 비싸요. This is more expensive.

다 "all" an adverb
　다 왔어요. We've arrived.

또 "also, again" used between sentences
　또 만나요. See you again.

도 "also" used after a noun
　내일도 시간이 없어요. I don't have time tomorrow either.

Track **127**

얼마 동안 여행했어요?

Jina	How was your trip this time?
Paul	It was really fun.
Jina	How long did you travel for?
Paul	I traveled for 3 days.
Jina	Where did you go?
Paul	I went to Jeju Island.
Jina	What did you do in Jeju Island?
Paul	I went hiking in the mountains. And I explored a little here and there.

지나   이번 여행이 어땠어요?

폴   정말 재미있었어요.

지나   얼마 동안 여행했어요?

폴   3일 동안 여행했어요.

지나   어디에 갔어요?

폴   제주도에 갔어요.

지나   제주도에서 뭐 했어요?

폴   등산했어요. 그리고 여기저기 구경했어요.

New Vocabulary

이번 this time
여행 travel, trip
얼마 동안 how long
여행하다 to go on a trip
동안 for (time duration)
제주도 Jeju Island
여기저기 here and there
구경하다 to look around

New Expressions

이번 여행이 어땠어요?
How was your trip this time?
얼마 동안 여행했어요?
How long did you travel for?
어디에 갔어요?
Where did you go?
뭐 했어요? What did you do?

Conversation Tips

★ **여행하다 = 여행 가다**
Both of these expressions are correct, but they take different markers:
제주도를 여행했어요. = 제주도에 여행 갔어요.

★ **Expressions for the length of a trip**
In the conversation above, "3일 동안 여행했어요." is a common expression used to talk about the duration of a trip, whether it be for business or pleasure. A trip of 3 days and 2 nights is referred to as 2박 3일 (이박 삼일). A day trip is called 당일 여행.

Track **128**

James	What did you do yesterday?
Rie	I toured Seoul.
James	What place did you like the best?
Rie	Namsan was the best.
James	How was it?
Rie	The scenery was beautiful.
James	What else did you do?
Rie	We had dinner at Insadong. And we also drank traditional tea.

제임스 　어제 뭐 했어요?

리에 　서울을 구경했어요.

제임스 　어디가 제일 좋았어요?

리에 　남산이 제일 좋았어요.

제임스 　어땠어요?

리에 　경치가 아름다웠어요.

제임스 　또 뭐 했어요?

리에 　인사동에서 저녁 식사를 했어요.
　　그리고 전통차도 마셨어요.

New Vocabulary

어제 yesterday

제일 most, best

좋다 to be good

남산 Namsan (famous mountain in Seoul)

경치 scenery

아름답다 to be beautiful

또 something else

인사동 Insadong (area of Seoul)

전통차 traditional tea

마시다 to drink

New Expressions

어제 뭐 했어요?
What did you do yesterday?

어디가 제일 좋았어요?
What place did you like the best?

어땠어요? How was it?

경치가 아름다웠어요.
The scenery was beautiful.

또 뭐 했어요?
What else did you do?

Conversation Tips

★ **서울을 구경했어요. "I toured Seoul."**
When using 구경하다 (to go sightseeing, to tour), the place that one went to sightsee or tour takes an object marker 을/를.

시내를 구경했어요. (O)　　I went sightseeing downtown.
시내에서 구경했어요. (x)

★ **저녁 식사(를) 하다 = 저녁(을) 먹다**
Use the verb 하다 with 저녁 식사 and the verb 먹다 with 저녁.

저녁 식사를 하다 (O)　　저녁을 먹다 (O)
저녁 식사를 먹다 (x)　　저녁을 하다 (x)

● 같이 [가치]

When the final consonants '⊏, ⋿' are followed by the vowel 'ㅣ', they are pronounced as [ㅈ,ㅊ] initial consonants in the next syllable.

(1) ⊏ → [ㅈ] 해돋이 [해도지], 굳이 [구지]
(2) ⋿ → [ㅊ] 밭이 [바치], 끝이 [끄치]

Additional Vocabulary

Track **130**

① ②  ③

1	옷을 입다	to put on clothes
2	신발을 신다	to put on shoes
3	사진을 찍다	to take a picture
4	한국어를 배우다	to learn Korean
5	영어를 가르치다	to teach English
6	선물을 주다	to give a present
7	웃다	to laugh
8	울다	to cry
9	친구를 기다리다	to wait for friends

④ ⑤ ⑥

생각하다	to think
선택하다	to choose
사용하다	to use
물어보다	to ask
대답하다	to answer, reply
걱정하다	to worry
잃어버리다	to lose
잊어버리다	to forget
찾다	to look for, find
받다	to receive
떠나다	to leave

⑦ ⑧ ⑨

Track 131

On the road

A What may I help you with?
B Please give me a map.
When requesting something from an information counter.

A May I help you?
B Yes, please help me.
When you're lost.

A Excuse me, but where is the ticket counter?
B Go this way.
When asking a bystander questions.

※ When the bystander will show you directly:
  이쪽으로 오세요. "Come this way."

Quiz Yourself!

Grammar

▶ Complete the sentence in the past tense. (1~3)

1　어제 집에서 책을 (1) ＿＿＿＿＿. 책이 (2) ＿＿＿＿＿.
　　　　　　　　　　　읽다　　　　　　　　재미있다

2　지난주에 마크 씨 집에서 파티를 (1) ＿＿＿. 파티에 사람들이 (2) ＿＿＿.
　　　　　　　　　　　　　　하다　　　　　　　　　　　많다

3　작년에 폴 씨가 한국에 (1) ＿＿＿. 그리고 한국어를 (2) ＿＿＿.
　　　　　　　　　　오다　　　　　　　　　　　배우다

▶ Look at the picture and complete the conversation. (4~6)

4　A 얼마 동안 잤어요?
　　B ＿＿＿＿＿ 동안 잤어요.

5　A 얼마 동안 여행했어요?
　　B ＿＿＿＿＿ 동안 여행했어요.

6　A 얼마 동안 한국어를 배웠어요?
　　B ＿＿＿＿＿ 배웠어요.

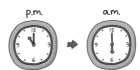

▶ Look at the picture and complete the conversation. (7~8)

7　A 산하고 바다 중에서 어디가 더 좋아요?
　　B ＿＿＿이/가 ＿＿＿보다 더 좋아요.

8　A 테니스하고 축구하고 농구 중에서 뭐가 제일 좋아요?
　　B ＿＿＿이/가 제일 좋아요.

산　　바다

테니스　　축구　　농구

y

y2

Listening

Track 132

▶ Listen and choose the correct answer. (9~10)

9 A 어제 제인 씨를 만났어요?

   B _____.

   ⓐ   ⓑ   ⓒ   ⓓ

10 A 냉면하고 비빔밥 중에서 뭐가 더 좋아요?

   B _____.

   ⓐ   ⓑ   ⓒ   ⓓ

Reading

▶ Read and choose the correct answer. (11~12)

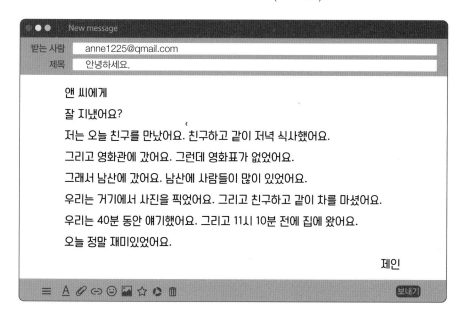

● ● ● New message

받는 사람 anne1225@qmail.com

제목 안녕하세요.

앤 씨에게

잘 지냈어요?

저는 오늘 친구를 만났어요. 친구하고 같이 저녁 식사했어요.

그리고 영화관에 갔어요. 그런데 영화표가 없었어요.

그래서 남산에 갔어요. 남산에 사람들이 많이 있었어요.

우리는 거기에서 사진을 찍었어요. 그리고 친구하고 같이 차를 마셨어요.

우리는 40분 동안 얘기했어요. 그리고 11시 10분 전에 집에 왔어요.

오늘 정말 재미있었어요.

제인

≡ A ✎ ⟷ ☺ 🖼 ☆ ♺ 🗑   보내기

11 제인 씨가 오늘 뭐 했어요?

   ⓐ 영화표를 샀어요.   ⓑ 혼자 차를 마셨어요.

   ⓒ 친구하고 점심 식사했어요.   ⓓ 남산에서 사진을 찍었어요.

12 제인 씨가 몇 시에 집에 왔어요?

   ⓐ 10시 40분   ⓑ 10시 50분   ⓒ 11시   ⓓ 11시 10분

Answers p.279

A Word on Culture

서해 Seohae

설악산 Seoraksan

한려수도 Hallyeosudo

진해 Jinhae

Q What are good places to visit in Korea?

Korea has four distinct seasons, and each season has its own natural beauty. So Korea is a country with many natural things to see. When spring comes around in March or April, the whole country becomes covered with spring flowers which start in the southern region. Yeosu is famous for camellia flowers, Jinhae for cherry blossom, and Gwangyang for plum trees. In Korea, 70% of the country's land is made up of mountains, so you can spot mountains everywhere, and the mystic scenery from the top of a green mountain in the summer is enough to captivate your heart. Also, Korea is surrounded by the sea on three sides of its land. People crowd together at the East Sea Beach, South Sea Hallyeosudo, and the West Sea tidal flat to avoid the heat during the summer. When autumn begins around October, the whole country is full of colorful autumn leaves. In particular, Naejangsan is the most breathtaking place to enjoy the splendor of autumn. In winter, people flock to the ski resorts of Gangwon-do. Those who want to feel a different atmosphere visit Jeju Island, which boasts natural scenery all year round.

Korea is also a country with many things to see culturally. If you want to experience a historical atmosphere, go to Gyeongju, the ancient capital a thousand years ago. You will be able to feel the culture of the time through old temples and historical sites in Gyeongju, the capital during the Silla period. If you want to know about the Confucian culture, take a look at Dosanseowon (a Confucian university in the past) and Hahoe Village in Andong. If you are interested in pottery or crafts, take a look at the Pottery Village in Icheon. If you want to feel the nature and culture of Korea, do not hesitate to go on a trip. For more information, visit the Korea Tourism Organization website: http://visitkorea.or.kr.

Chapter 15   내일 한국 음식을 만들 거예요.

- The informal polite form of the verbs -(으)ㄹ 거예요 in the future tense
- Negating with 못 "cannot"

내일 뭐 할 거예요?
What are you going to do tomorrow?

친구를 만날 거예요.
I am going to meet a friend.

● The informal polite form of the verbs -(으)ㄹ 거예요 in the future tense

In order to form the future tense, use the following grammar patterns.

ending in a vowel	ending in a consonant
내일 여행 갈 거예요.	내일 책을 읽을 거예요.
I am going on a trip tomorrow.	I am going to read a book tomorrow.

이번 주에 너무 바빴어요. 그래서 이번 주말에 집에서 쉴 거예요.

I was so busy this week. So I'm going to rest at home this weekend.

For adjectives, this pattern can imply a guess or slight uncertainty, like "will probably/am probably going to…." To make the meaning more clear, use the word 아마 "probably."

ending in a vowel	ending in a consonant
마크 씨가 아마 바쁠 거예요.	지나 씨가 아마 기분이 좋을 거예요.
Mark is probably going to be busy.	Jina is probably going to be in a good mood.

In 'ㄷ' irregular verbs, the 'ㄷ' becomes 'ㄹ' whenever the verb tense begins with a vowel (such as -을 거예요).

내일 음악을 들을 거예요.   I am going to listen to music tomorrow.

In 'ㅂ' irregular verbs, the 'ㅂ' becomes 우 whenever the verb tense begins with a vowel (such as -을 거예요).

이번 시험이 어려울 거예요.   This test will be hard.

* Refer to page 269 for examples of irregular verbs.

다음 주 주말에 같이 여행 가요.
Let's go traveling together next weekend.

미안해요. 못 가요.
I'm sorry. I cannot go.

Negating with 못 "cannot"

When you want to express that the subject can't do something for some reason, use 못 "cannot." 못 is used with verbs. The placement of 못 in the sentence is the same as the placement of 안.

하다 **verbs**	other action verbs
일 못 해요.	못 자요.
운동 못 해요.	못 먹어요.

오늘 시간 없어요. 그래서 운동 못 해요.
I have no time today. So I can't exercise.

어제 커피를 많이 마셨어요. 그래서 못 잤어요.
I drank a lot of coffee yesterday. So I couldn't sleep.

The placement of 안 and 못

	하다 **verbs**	the other action verbs
안 **do not**	일 안 해요.	안 가요.
못 **cannot**	일 못 해요.	못 가요.

	하다 **adjectives**	the other adjectives
안 **do not**	안 피곤해요.	안 비싸요.
못 **cannot**	You cannot use 못 with adjectives.	

Yujin	What are you going to do tomorrow?
James	Nothing special. Why?
Yujin	That's good.
	Tomorrow we are going to make Korean food at home.
	Let's make it together.
James	What time are you going to make it tomorrow?
Yujin	We are going to make it around 2 in the afternoon?
James	OK, see you tomorrow.

유진	내일 뭐 할 거예요?
제임스	별일 없어요. 왜요?
유진	잘됐어요.
	내일 우리 집에서 한국 음식을 만들 거예요.
	같이 만들어요.
제임스	내일 언제 만들 거예요?
유진	오후 2시쯤 만들 거예요.
제임스	알겠어요. 내일 봐요.

New Vocabulary

내일 tomorrow
별일 a particular thing
우리 our
우리 집 my house

New Expressions

내일 뭐 할 거예요?
What are you going to do tomorrow?
별일 없어요. Nothing special.
잘됐어요. That's good.
알겠어요. OK./I understand.
내일 봐요. See you tomorrow.

Conversation Tips

★ **잘됐어요 "That's great./That's good./That turned out well."**
잘됐어요 is used when meeting expectations or when you hear good news. On the other hand, when something doesn't meet your expectations or you hear bad news, you can say 안됐어요. If you would like to convey a sense of surprise, use the ending -네요 as in 잘됐네요 or 안됐네요.

1 A	제인 씨가 회사에 취직했어요.	Jane got a job at the office.
B	잘됐어요. (= 잘됐네요.)	That's good. (with surprise)
2 A	폴 씨가 시험에 떨어졌어요.	Paul failed his test.
B	안됐어요. (= 안됐네요.)	I'm sorry to hear that. (with surprise)

Jina	Mark, I'm going to go to Ann's house next Friday. Let's go together.
Mark	I'm sorry. I can't go.
Jina	Why? Do you have something going on?
Mark	I'm going to Japan on a business trip next Thursday.
Jina	Oh, is that right? How long will you be there?
Mark	I'll be there for 5 days.
Jina	I understand. Have a good business trip, then.

지나 마크 씨, 다음 주 금요일에 앤 씨 집에 갈 거예요. 같이 가요.

마크 미안해요. 못 가요.

지나 왜요? 무슨 일이 있어요?

마크 다음 주 목요일에 일본에 출장 갈 거예요.

지나 그래요? 얼마 동안 거기에 있을 거예요?

마크 5일 동안 있을 거예요.

지나 네, 알겠어요. 그럼, 출장 잘 다녀오세요.

New Vocabulary

다음 주 next week
못 cannot
무슨 what
일 something
목요일 Thursday
일본 Japan
출장 business trip
출장 가다 to go on a business trip
거기 there
있다 to be, stay
잘 well
다녀오다 to go and return

New Expressions

같이 가요. Let's go together.
미안해요. I'm sorry.
무슨 일이 있어요?
Is there something wrong?
얼마 동안 거기에 있을 거예요?
How long will you be there?
출장 잘 다녀오세요.
Have a good business trip.

Conversation Tips

★ 미안해요 "I'm sorry."

In English, the phrase "I'm sorry" is used for apologies and also to express pity, disappointment, or regret. But in Korean, "미안해요." is just used for apologies. In English, for instance, you might say, "I'm sorry for your loss." Here you're not apologizing for anything, but instead expressing regret or pity. In this case, in Korean, the appropriate expression is "유감이에요."

Track 135

● 못 해요 [모 태요], 못 먹어요 [몬 머거요]

1. The final consonant '△' in 못 is pronounced as [ㄷ]; however, when combined with the initial consonant 'ㅎ', the [ㄷ] and 'ㅎ' are pronounced together as [ㅌ].

못 했어요 [모 태써요]

2. The final consonant '△' in 못 is pronounced as [ㄷ]; however when followed by the initial consonant 'ㄴ' or 'ㅁ' it is pronounced as [ㄴ].

못 나가요 [몬 나가요], 못 마셔요 [몬 마셔요]

Additional Vocabulary

Track 136

크다 ↔ 작다
to be big ↔ small

춥다 ↔ 덥다
to be cold ↔ hot

키가 크다 ↔ 키가 작다
to be tall ↔ short

길다 ↔ 짧다
to be long ↔ short

가깝다 ↔ 멀다
to be near ↔ far

재미있다 ↔ 재미없다
to be interesting ↔ uninteresting
to be fun ↔ boring

같다 ↔ 다르다
to be the same ↔ different

비싸다 ↔ 싸다
to be expensive ↔ cheap

좋다 ↔ 나쁘다
to be good ↔ bad

많다 ↔ 적다
to be many ↔ few

배고프다 ↔ 배부르다
to be hungry ↔ full

어렵다 ↔ 쉽다
to be difficult ↔ easy

조용하다 ↔ 시끄럽다
to be quiet ↔ loud

가볍다 ↔ 무겁다
to be light ↔ heavy

깨끗하다 ↔ 더럽다
to be clean ↔ dirty

뚱뚱하다 ↔ 마르다
to be fat ↔ skinny

어둡다 ↔ 밝다
to be dark ↔ bright

Expressions when reacting to news

A Jane passed the test.
B That's great.
When you hear good news about someone.

A Jinsu failed his test.
B I'm sorry to hear that.
When you hear bad news about someone.

A That's fortunate.
When something that worried you ends well.

A Oh, no!
When you hear about something that worries you.

Grammar

▶ Choose the correct answer to complete the sentence. (1~4)

1 작년에 수영을 배웠어요. 내년에 태권도를 (ⓐ 배웠어요. / ⓑ 배울 거예요.)

2 조금 전에 물을 (ⓐ 마셨어요. / ⓑ 마실 거예요.) 그래서 지금 물을 안 마실 거예요.

3 어제 서울 여기저기를 (ⓐ 걸었어요. / ⓑ 걸을 거예요.) 오늘 집에서 쉴 거예요.

4 내일 고향에 돌아갈 거예요. 앞으로 1년 동안 고향에서 (ⓐ 살았어요. / ⓑ 살 거예요.)

▶ Complete the sentence -으(ㄹ) 거예요 in the future tense. (5~7)

5 오늘 친구를 만나요. 내일도 친구를 _____.

6 이번 주말에 한국어 책을 읽어요. 다음 주말에도 한국어 책을 _____.

7 이번 달에 영화를 봐요. 다음 달에도 영화를 _____.

▶ Complete the conversation as shown in the example below. (8~9)

Ex. A 내일 같이 여행 가요.
     B 미안해요. <u>같이 여행 못 가요</u>. 요즘 너무 바빠요.

8 A 같이 영화 봐요.
   B 미안해요. _____. 다른 약속이 있어요.

9 A 같이 술 마셔요.
   B 미안해요. _____. 감기에 걸렸어요.

▶ Listen to the question and choose the correct answer. (10~11)

Track 138

10 ⓐ 친구 집에 갈 거예요.

ⓑ 친구 생일이 아니에요.

ⓒ 친구를 안 만날 거예요.

ⓓ 내일이 5월 20일이에요.

11 ⓐ 여행 시간이 많아요.

ⓑ 기차표를 살 거예요.

ⓒ 다른 약속이 있어요.

ⓓ 여행사에서 일 안 해요.

Reading

▶ Read and choose the correct answer. (12~13)

12

> 마크 씨는 회사원이에요. 회사가 서울에 있어요.
>
> 그런데 내일은 회사에 안 가요. 왜냐하면 부산에서 회의가 있어요.
>
> 그래서 내일 마크 씨가 부산에 _____.

ⓐ 안 갈 거예요

ⓑ 출장 갈 거예요

ⓒ 여행 갈 거예요

ⓓ 이사 갈 거예요

13

> 한국에서 여섯 달 동안 일했어요. 너무 바빴어요. 한국어를 _____.
>
> 그래서 한국어를 잘 못해요. 다음 달부터 한국어를 공부할 거예요.

ⓐ 공부했어요

ⓑ 공부할 거예요

ⓒ 공부 못 했어요

ⓓ 공부 못 할 거예요

Answers p.290

A Word on Culture

Q **What kind of presents do Koreans give on different occasions?**

Gift giving is guided as much by culture as by personality. What kinds of gifts do Koreans give? When Koreans visit their friends' houses, they often bring fruit. On the other hand, when visiting a friend at work, Koreans often bring bottled juice.

For a housewarming party, Koreans usually give soap or toilet paper. Soap has a particular meaning – it is hoped that fortune will rise in your family as the soap bubbles rise in the air. Newlyweds moving into their first apartment usually receive enough soap and toilet paper for at least their first year together.

If you should attend a friend's baby's first birthday party, the typical present is a gold ring. Most Koreans still have a gold ring or two from their own first birthdays. These days, some people will give money rather than a gold ring, but the first birthday is still associated with gold rings. You can find special "first birthday" gold rings at almost any jewelry shop.

Students with a big exam ahead usually receive 엿 (a toffee-like candy) or 찹쌀떡 (a food made from sticky rice). In Korean, the verb "to pass" (붙다) sounds like the verb "to stick" (붙다) so students receive sticky presents such as these.

At big events such as weddings or funerals Koreans usually prepare envelopes of money. This tradition comes from a communal past when people exchanged labor with one another in turn. When one family had a big event or crisis, others would contribute money or labor, knowing that if later they should need help, others would return the favor. If you should happen to attend a wedding or a funeral, you will easily find the person in the reception area whose duty it is to receive envelopes of money from the guests. Bring on the gifts!

Chapter 16 같이 영화 보러 갈 수 있어요?

- -(으)ㄹ 수 있다/없다 "can/cannot"
- -(으)러 가다/오다 "to go/come in order to (verb)"
- Expressing strong intent -(으)ㄹ게요 "I will"

태권도 할 수 있어요?
Can you do Taekwondo?

네, 할 수 있어요.
Yes, I can.

● -(으)ㄹ 수 있다/없다 "can/cannot"

-(으)ㄹ 수 있다 is used to indicate whether someone is able to do some action. The negative (unable to do) is -(으)ㄹ 수 없다.

	ending in a vowel	ending in a consonant
positive	할 수 있어요. I can do it.	읽을 수 있어요. I can read.
negative	할 수 없어요. I can't do it.	읽을 수 없어요. I can't read.

1 A 운전할 수 있어요? Can you drive?
   B 네, 운전할 수 있어요. Yes, I can drive.

2 A 이 음식을 혼자 다 먹을 수 있어요? Can you eat all this food by yourself?
   B 아니요, 먹을 수 없어요. No, I can't eat it all.

When forming sentences of different tenses, just change the endings of 있다/없다.

past 읽을 수 있었어요. I could read it.

future 읽을 수 있을 거예요. I will be able to read it.

? I wonder...

못 is a grammar that has a negative meaning, which is often used instead of -(으)ㄹ 수 없다. 못 is combined only with a verb, and the position where 못 is used is the same as where 안 is used.

A 수영할 수 있어요? Can you swim?
B 아니요, 수영할 수 없어요. No, I cannot swim.
    (= 수영 못 해요. I cannot swim.)

같이 축구 보러 **가요**. 제가 표 **살게요**.
Let's go see a soccer game. I'll buy the tickets.

네, 그래요.
Yes, sure.

-(으)러 가다/오다 "to go/come in order to (verb)"

-(으)러 가다/오다 is used when you are going or coming to a place in order to do something.

ending in a vowel	ending in a consonant
친구를 만나러 가요. I am going to meet a friend.	점심을 먹으러 가요. I am going to eat lunch.

A 왜 친구 집에 가요?   Why are you going to a friend's house?
B 공부하러 가요.   I'm going (in order) to study.

When changing tenses in sentences, just change the endings of 가다/오다.

past   일하러 왔어요.   I came (in order) to work.
future   옷을 사러 갈 거예요.   I will go (in order) to buy clothes.

Expressing strong intent -(으)ㄹ게요 "I will"

When you want to emphasize your determination or intent to do something to the listener, use the pattern -(으)ㄹ게요. This pattern can only be used with a single subject "I" and cannot be used to form a question.

ending in a vowel	ending in a consonant
먼저 갈게요. I will go first.	먹을게요. I will eat it.

A 뭐 먹을 거예요?   What are you going to eat?
B 갈비 먹을게요.   I'll eat Galbi.

Jane	Can you swim?
Jinsu	No.
Jane	Then, can you play tennis?
Jinsu	I can play. But I can't play well.
Jane	That's OK. I will teach you. Let's go play tennis tomorrow.
Jinsu	Sounds good.

제인   수영할 수 있어요?

진수   아니요.

제인   그럼, 테니스 칠 수 있어요?

진수   칠 수 있어요. 그런데 잘 못해요.

제인   괜찮아요. 제가 가르쳐 줄게요.
        내일 같이 테니스 치러 가요.

진수   좋아요.

New Vocabulary

수영하다 to swim
테니스 tennis
테니스(를) 치다 to play tennis
못하다 to be bad, poor
제가 I
괜찮다 to be fine, okay
가르쳐 주다 to teach

New Expressions

잘 못해요 I can't do it well.
(an expression of modesty)
괜찮아요. It's OK.
제가 가르쳐 줄게요.
I'll teach you.
내일 같이 테니스 치러 가요.
Let's go play tennis tomorrow.

Conversation Tips

★ **The singular subject 제가 vs. 저는**

There are two ways to express the singular subject "I" in Korean: 제가 (with the subject marker 이/가) and 저는 (with the marker 은/는). Although the subject marker is used most frequently, remember that if you want to emphasize "I" as a new topic (such as when introducing yourself), or stress some difference, you should use a topic marker. But without this specific context, with the pattern -(으)ㄹ게요, you can usually use 제가.

어제 제가 (= 저는) 친구를 만났어요. Yesterday I met a friend.

제가 (≠ 저는) 할게요. I will do it.

James	Do you have time this Saturday?
Jina	Why?
James	I have two movie tickets. Can we go to see a movie together?
Jina	I'm sorry. I have another appointment.
James	I understand. Let's go together next time.
Jina	I'm really sorry.

제임스 이번 주 토요일에 시간 있어요?

지나 왜요?

제임스 영화표가 두 장 있어요.

같이 영화 보러 갈 수 있어요?

지나 미안해요. 다른 약속이 있어요.

제임스 알겠어요. 다음에 같이 가요.

지나 정말 미안해요.

New Vocabulary

토요일 Saturday

영화표 movie ticket

다른 different, another

약속 appointment

New Expressions

이번 주 토요일에 시간 있어요?
Do you have time this Saturday?

같이 영화 보러 갈 수 있어요?
Can we go to see a movie together?

다른 약속이 있어요.
I have another appointment.

다음에 같이 가요.
Let's go together next time.

정말 미안해요. I'm really sorry.

Conversation Tips

★ **다음에 "next time"**
When you find it difficult to make plans with someone and want to express interest in meeting at another time, you can use the expression 다음에 "next time." Like the English expression, "well, maybe next time," this doesn't refer to a specific date or time.

★ **알겠어요 "I understand." vs. 알아요 "I know."**
알겠어요 means "I understand" while 알아요 means "I know." In the above conversation, since B realizes that A has an appointment, B uses 알겠어요.

● 좋아요 [조아요]

When a final consonant ' ㅎ ' is followed by a vowel, ' ㅎ ' is silent.

(1) 많이 [마니]
(2) 괜찮아요 [괜차나요]

Additional Vocabulary

Track 142

The verb 치다 means "to hit" and is used with 테니스 "tennis," 탁구 "table tennis," 피아노 "piano".

테니스를 치다   탁구를 치다   피아노를 치다

The verb 타다 "to ride" is used with 스케이트 "skate," 스키 "ski," 자전거 "bicycle".

스케이트를 타다   스키를 타다   자전거를 타다

The verb 하다 is used with team sports: 축구 "soccer," 농구 "basketball," 태권도 "taekwondo".

축구를 하다   농구를 하다   태권도를 하다

Track **143**

Accepting an invitation

A When do you have time?
B Anytime is OK.

Other expressions
어디든지. "Anywhere."
뭐든지. "Anything."
누구든지. "Anybody."

Declining an invitation

A Let's have lunch together.
B I'm sorry, (I can't.)

(1) I don't have time.
(2) I have a lot of work to do.
(3) I have another appointment.
(4) I'm not feeling well.

Grammar

▶ Look at the picture and choose the correct answer. (1~3)

테니스 치다　　　　축구하다　　　　스키 타다

1 폴 씨가 테니스 칠 수 (ⓐ 있어요. / ⓑ 없어요.)

2 폴 씨가 축구할 수 (ⓐ 있어요. / ⓑ 없어요.)

3 폴 씨가 스키 탈 수 (ⓐ 있어요. / ⓑ 없어요.)

▶ Choose the correct answer to complete the conversation. (4~7)

4　A　왜 식당에 가요?

　　B　ⓐ 운동하러 식당에 가요.

　　　　ⓑ 점심을 먹으러 식당에 가요.

5　A　왜 회사에 가요?

　　B　ⓐ 쉬러 회사에 가요.

　　　　ⓑ 일하러 회사에 가요.

6　A　왜 영화관에 가요?

　　B　ⓐ 요리하러 영화관에 가요.

　　　　ⓑ 영화를 보러 영화관에 가요.

7　A　왜 학교에 가요?

　　B　ⓐ 옷을 사러 가요.

　　　　ⓑ 한국어를 배우러 가요.

▶ Choose the correct answer to complete the conversation. (8~9)

8　A　비빔밥이 조금 매워요.

　　B　그래요? 그럼, 다른 음식을 (ⓐ 먹을게요. / ⓑ 먹을 수 없어요.)

9　A　다음 주에 같이 영화 봐요.

　　B　미안해요, (ⓐ 같이 영화 볼게요. / ⓑ 같이 영화 볼 수 없어요.)

Listening

▶ Listen and choose the correct answer to complete the sentence. (10~11)

Track 144

10 일본어로 얘기할 수 있어요. 그래서 _____.

ⓐ   ⓑ   ⓒ   ⓓ

11 자동차를 운전할 수 없어요. 그래서 _____.

ⓐ   ⓑ   ⓒ   ⓓ

Reading

▶ Read and choose the correct answer .

> 안녕하세요? 저는 제인이에요. 캐나다 대학교에서 1년 동안 한국어를
> 공부했어요. 그래서 한국어를 조금 할 수 있어요. 한국 문화를 공부하러
> 한국에 왔어요.
>
> 저는 한국 음식을 정말 좋아해요. 김치하고 비빔밥, 매운 음식도 다 먹을
> 수 있어요. 하지만 한국 음식을 만들 수 없어요. 그래서 다음 주에 한국
> 요리를 배우러 요리 학원에 갈 거예요.

12   뭐가 맞아요?

ⓐ 제인 씨가 여행하러 한국에 왔어요.

ⓑ 제인 씨가 한국 요리를 배울 거예요.

ⓒ 제인 씨가 한국 음식을 먹을 수 없어요.

ⓓ 제인 씨가 대학교에서 한국어를 가르쳤어요.

Answers p.280

A Word on Culture

Q Have you heard the phrase, "modesty is a virtue"?

Ask a Korean if he can speak English, and even if he can speak it well, he will reply politely that he cannot. And if he really can't speak well? Of course, if he really can't speak well he will say the same thing. But in Korea, for the most case, there is only one way to demonstrate modesty in such a situation, and that is with the phrase, "잘 못해요" (I don't speak well).

Koreans consider modesty very important, especially in interactions with people to whom they need to show respect. While in the West, honesty is very important, in Korea, modesty is more important than honesty. In Korean society, it is the skilled person who acts modest in front of others who are seen as considerate and wise, rather than the skilled person who displays his talents. That's why people say "잘 못해요"(I can't do it well); they know as well as others that they, in fact, can do it well, but need to display a sense of modesty at all the times.

However, in a job interview or similar situation, unpracticed at bragging, Koreans can sound as if they are incompetent. The same phrase can sound like modesty or incompetence depending on the situation.

So now you know – next time a Korean praises your ability to speak Korean, modesty reply "잘 못해요!"

Chapter 17 미안하지만, 다시 한번 말해 주세요.

⊞ -아/어 주세요 "Please do (verb) for me."

⊞ Confirming information -요?

좀 천천히 말**해** 주세요.
Please speak more slowly.

● **-아/어 주세요** "Please do (verb) for me."

You can use -아/어 주세요 to make a polite request. When -아/어 주세요 is combined with the verb stem ending in 하, it becomes 해 주세요. If the ending of the verb stem ends with the vowel '아' or '오', -아 주세요 is used. Otherwise, -어 주세요 is used. When asking for a noun, just add 주세요 to the noun.

Present				
말하다	말하	+ -여 주세요	→	말해 주세요
찾다	찾	+ -아 주세요	→	찾아 주세요
기다리다	기다리	+ -어 주세요	→	기다려 주세요

> **! Be careful**
> 도와주세요.
> Please help me.

길을 가르쳐 주세요.	Please teach me how to go there.
여기로 와 주세요.	Please come here.
이름을 써 주세요.	Please write down your name.
전화해 주세요.	Please call me.

Using the word 좀 ("please") when making a request conveys courtesy. If the sentence has no object, use 좀 at the beginning of the sentence. Otherwise, use 좀 after the object, instead of the object marker 을/를.

좀 자세히 말해 주세요.	Please speak in detail.
사진 좀 찍어 주세요.	Please take a picture for me.
영수증 좀 주세요.	Please give me a receipt.
물 좀 주세요.	Please give me some water.

내일 명동에서 만나요.
Let's meet tomorrow at Myeongdong

? 네? 명동요?
What? Myeongdong?

● Confirming information 요?

If you didn't hear something well or want to confirm what you heard is correct, you can use 요? after the noun you wish to confirm or repeat. Technically, 요? is attached to a noun regardless of whether it ends in a vowel or a consonant. However, in reality, you can hear 이요? often after a noun that ends in a consonant. 네? is often used in these circumstances to indicate that something was not heard clearly.

1 A 영화가 11시에 시작해요.   The movie starts at 11.

   B 네? 몇 시요? 11시요?   What? What time? 11?

2 A 여권이 필요해요.   You need your passport.

   B 여권요?   My passport?

With close friends or people of lesser status (much younger people, for instance) you can just ask 11시? or 여권? without the ending 요?. But, in all other cases, you need to use the ending 요?.

※ When you didn't hear something clearly and want to ask a short clarifying question, use the following:

Who?	When?	Where?	Why?	How?	What?
누구요?	언제요?	어디요?	왜요?	어떻게요?	뭐요?

Track **145**

내일 5시에 강남역 7번 출구…

다시 한번 말해 주세요.

Jina	Let's meet at 5:00 tomorrow at Gangnam subway station, exit number 7.
Paul	What? I didn't hear you. I'm sorry but please say it again.
Jina	Meet at 5:00 tomorrow at Myeongdong subway station, exit number 7.
Paul	At what exit number?
Jina	Exit number 7.
Paul	OK, I understand.

지나   내일 5시에 강남역 7번 출구에서 만나요.

폴   네? 잘 못 들었어요.
미안하지만, 다시 한번 말해 주세요.

지나   내일 5시에 강남역 7번 출구에서 만나요.

폴   몇 번 출구요?

지나   7번 출구요.

폴   네, 알겠어요.

New Vocabulary

강남 Gangnam

7번 number 7

출구 exit

만나다 to meet

듣다 to listen to, to hear

다시 again

다시 한번 once more

말하다 to speak

New Expressions

네? What?

잘 못 들었어요.
I didn't hear you.

미안하지만, I'm sorry but ...

다시 한번 말해 주세요.
Please say it again.

몇 번 출구요?
At what exit number?

Conversation Tips

★ **Using 못**

In Korean, when negating verbs 보다 "to see" and 듣다 "to hear" use 못 rather than 안. Although in English you would say "I didn't hear you" and "I didn't see you," in Korean, you would say "못 들었어요." and "못 봤어요."

A   마크 씨 봤어요?   Did you see Mark?
B   아니요, 못 봤어요.   No, I don't see him.

Track 146

30분쯤
기다려 주세요.

알겠어요.

Mark	Hello.
Ann	Mark, this is Ann.
Mark	Ann, where are you right now?
Ann	I'm on the bus. I'm sorry. I'm stuck in traffic.
Mark	Oh, really? About what time will you arrive?
Ann	Please wait about 30 minutes.
Mark	OK. I will wait.

마크   여보세요.

앤   마크 씨, 저 앤이에요.

마크   앤 씨, 지금 어디에 있어요?

앤   지금 버스에 있어요.
미안해요. 길이 너무 많이 막혀요.

마크   그래요? 언제쯤 도착할 수 있어요?

앤   30분쯤 기다려 주세요.

마크   알겠어요. 기다릴게요.

New Vocabulary

길 road
너무 많이 too much (many)
막히다 to be blocked
도착하다 to arrive
기다리다 to wait

New Expressions

여보세요. Hello.

지금 어디에 있어요?
Where are you now?

길이 너무 많이 막혀요.
I'm stuck in traffic.

언제쯤 도착할 수 있어요?
About what time will you arrive?

30분쯤 기다려 주세요.
Please wait about 30 minutes.

기다릴게요. I will wait.

Conversation Tips

★ 여보세요. **"Hello." (on the phone)**
This greeting is only used when beginning a phone conversation.

★ 저 앤이에요. **"This is Ann."**
When introducing yourself on the phone, you can drop the marker 는.

A   여보세요.   Hello.
B   폴 씨, 저(는) 유진이에요. Paul, this is Yujin.

Pronunciation

Track 147

● 의자 [의자], 편의점 [펴니점], 친구의 책 [친구에 책]

The pronunciation of 의 changes depending upon its location.

1. When 의 occurs in the first syllable of a word, it is pronounced as written.

    의사 [의사]

2. When 의 occurs in the second syllable, it can be pronounced as [이].

    수의사 [수이사]

3. When 의 is used as a possessive, it can be pronounced as [에].

    선생님의 가방 [선생니메 가방]

Additional Vocabulary

Track 148

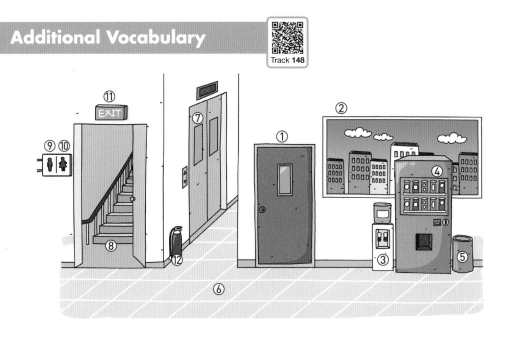

1	문	door	5	휴지통	garbage can	9	남자 화장실	the men's room
2	창문	window	6	복도	hall	10	여자 화장실	the ladies' room
3	정수기	water purifier	7	엘리베이터	elevator	11	비상구	emergency exit
4	자판기	vending machine	8	계단	stairs	12	소화기	fire extinguisher

Expressions frequently used by foreigners

A   Please speak slowly.

A   Please speak loudly.

A   Please tell me one more time.

A   Please speak in English.

Grammar

▶ Connect the appropriate sentences and complete the sentence as shown in the example below. (1~3)

Ex. 전화번호를 몰라요. •

1 잘 못 들었어요. •

2 오늘 돈이 없어요. •

3 5분 후에 갈 거예요. •

• ⓐ 잠깐 _____. (기다리다)

• ⓑ 돈을 _____. (빌리다)

• ⓒ 전화번호를 <u>가르쳐 주세요</u>. (가르치다)

• ⓓ 다시 한번 _____. (얘기하다)

▶ Look at the picture and complete the conversation. (4~5)

4 A 요즘 태권도를 배워요.

　B 네? _____?

5 A 다음 주에 시험이 있어요.

　B 네? _____?

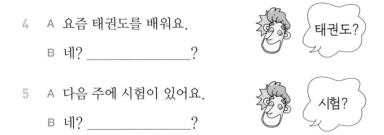

▶ Complete the conversation by using 못. (6~9)

6 A 여행 얘기 들었어요?

　B 아니요, _____.

7 A 마크 씨 봤어요?

　B 아니요, _____.

8 A 뉴스 들었어요?

　B 아니요, _____.

9 A 새 영화 봤어요?

　B 아니요, _____.

▶ Listen and choose the correct answer to complete the sentence. (10~12)

Track **150**

10　너무 빨리 말해요. 그래서 잘 못들었어요. _____.

　　ⓐ　　　　　　　ⓑ　　　　　　　ⓒ　　　　　　　ⓓ

11　테니스를 잘쳐요? 저는 잘 못 쳐요. _____.

　　ⓐ　　　　　　　ⓑ　　　　　　　ⓒ　　　　　　　ⓓ

12　전화번호를 알아요. 하지만 지금 전화할 수 없어요. _____.

　　ⓐ　　　　　　　ⓑ　　　　　　　ⓒ　　　　　　　ⓓ

Reading

▶ Read and mark the letters in the correct order.

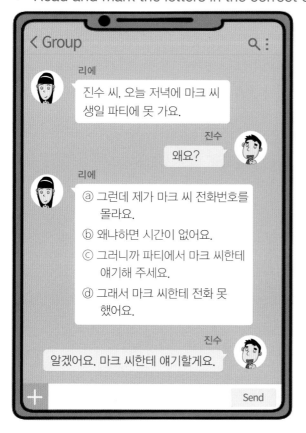

13　(　ⓑ　)

　　↓

　　(　　　)

　　↓

　　(　　　)

　　↓

　　(　　　)

Answers p.290

A Word on Culture

Q How should you speak to a stranger?

How should you speak to someone you don't know? Since Koreans rarely use the term "you," should you just roughly guess someone's age and call all older people 할머니 (grandmother) or 할아버지 (grandfather), all middle-aged people 아줌마 (aunt, ma'am) or 아저씨 (mister/uncle) and all young people 학생 (student)? The answer is no.

If you need to speak to a stranger in a public place, such as the street or subway, it's best to address him indirectly and avoid guessing an appropriate title. Begin with "저" or "저기요" and once you have the person's attention, you may begin speaking.

In a restaurant, however, get your server's attention by waving your hand and saying "여기요." This method works for flagging a taxi as well. In these cases, it's fine to speak loudly to make sure you get the waiter or taxi driver's attention.

But otherwise, stick with "저기요" for strangers. This way you can avoid all of those problematic titles!

Chapter 18 저도 한국어를 배우고 싶어요.

- -고 싶다 "to want to (verb)"
- Questions with -지 않아요? "isn't it?"
- The grammar pattern for meaning attempting -아/어 보다
  "to try to (verb)"

제주도에 가고 **싶어요**.
I want to go to Jeju Island.

그런데 거기 날씨가 덥**지 않아요**?
But isn't the weather there hot?

● **-고 싶다** "to want to (verb)"

-고 싶다 is used to express a desire to do something. Put -고 싶다 after the verb stem.

A   어디에서 저녁 먹고 싶어요?   Where do you want to eat dinner?

B   한국 식당에서 먹고 싶어요.   I want to eat at a Korean restaurant.

To change the tense, just change 싶다.

past   어제 친구를 만나고 싶었어요. 그런데 못 만났어요.
        I wanted to meet my friend yesterday. But I couldn't meet her.

future   다시 보고 싶을 거예요.   I'll want to see her again.

● Questions with **-지 않아요?** "isn't it?"

There are two basic ways to make a negative sentence in Korean – use 안 in front of the verb (as we learned in chapter 13), or use -지 않다 after the verb stem. Although there is no difference in meaning, people tend to use the short negation of 안 in speaking and the grammar pattern -지 않다 in writing.

This grammar pattern -지 않다 also has another use; it is a polite way to ask for assurance with a short question. In English, if someone offers to walk you to the subway station, you might say, "Aren't you busy?" or "Isn't it cold?". This pattern performs a similar function in Korean.

ending in a vowel	ending in a consonant
바쁘지 않아요?	춥지 않아요?
Aren't you busy?	Isn't it cold?

혹시 경주에 **가** 봤어요?
By any chance,
have you been to Gyeongju?

네, 폴 씨도 한번 **가** 보세요.
Yes, Paul, you should go.

● The grammar pattern for meaning attempting -아/어 보다
"to try to (verb)"

This pattern is used to describe an attempt at some action or behavior. -아/어 보다 is only combined with a verb. If the stem of the verb ends in 하, it becomes 해 보다, and when the stem ends with the vowel 'ㅏ' or 'ㅗ', -아 보다 is used. In other cases, -어 보다 is used. The following three patterns are all derived from -아/어 보다.

1. **-아/어 봤다** to have (done something)

> 먹다   먹 + -어 봤다   →   먹어 봤다 have tried (something)

A 경주에 가 봤어요?   Have you ever been to Gyeongju?

B 네, 한번 가 봤어요.   Yes, I've been there once.

  아니요, 아직 못 가 봤어요.   No, I haven't been there yet.

2. **-아/어 보세요** Try it (Give it a try)

> 먹다   먹 + -어 보세요   →   먹어 보세요 Try it (You should try it.)

A 경주에 아직 못 가 봤어요.   I have not been to Gyeongju yet.

B 경주가 정말 좋아요. 꼭 가 보세요.   I really like Gyeongju. You have to go.
                                                 (lit. Try to visit there.)

3. **-아/어 볼게요** will try it

> 먹다   먹 + -어 볼게요   →   먹어 볼게요 I will try it.

A 한국 치킨이 맛있어요. 한번 먹어 보세요.   Korean chicken is delicious. Try it.

B 네, 먹어 볼게요.   Yes, I will try it.

The grammar pattern -어 보다 cannot be combined with 보다 ("to see"). Rather, just 보다 is used, such as 봤어요("I have seen it"), 보세요 ("You should see it"), 볼게요 ("I will try it"). (Ex. 한국 영화 봐 봤어요.(X) → 한국 영화 봤어요.(○))

Track 151

저도 한국어를 배우고 싶어요.

한번 시작해 보세요.

James	How are you doing these days?
Jane	I'm doing well. I'm learning Korean these days.
James	Oh, really? I also want to learn Korean. But isn't it difficult?
Jane	It's not difficult. It's fun. James, you should give it a try.
James	Yes, I'll give it a try.

제임스   요즘 어떻게 지내요?

제인   잘 지내요. 요즘 한국어를 배워요.

제임스   그래요? 저도 한국어를 배우고 싶어요.
그런데 한국어가 어렵지 않아요?

제인   안 어려워요. 재미있어요.
제임스 씨도 한번 시작해 보세요.

제임스   네, 한번 해 볼게요.

New Vocabulary

지내다 to get along, pass time
어렵다 to be difficult
시작하다 to begin, start

New Expressions

요즘 어떻게 지내요?
How are you doing these days?
잘 지내요. I'm doing well.
어렵지 않아요? Isn't it difficult?
한번 시작해 보세요. Give it a try.
한번 해 볼게요. I'll give it a try.

Conversation Tips

★ **요즘 어떻게 지내요? "How are you doing these days?"**
This phrase is commonly used at the beginning of a conversation with someone you haven't seen in a while. It is typically answered by "잘 지내요." ("I'm doing well.").

★ **Using 한번 for persuasion**
한번 ("once") is often used in front of the verb when asking someone to try something. It is often used as a request, similar to "give it a try" in English.

Track 152

Yujin	What are you doing now?
Mark	I want to go on a trip to the mountains or the sea. So I am looking for a travel destination.
Yujin	Mark, have you ever been to Jeju Island?
Mark	No, I have not been there yet.
Yujin	Then, you should go to Jeju Island. The view is really nice.
Mark	Yes, I will go to Jeju Island. By the way, what is famous in Jeju Island?
Yujin	Seafood cuisine is famous.
Mark	Really? Thanks a lot.

유진   지금 뭐 해요?

마크   산이나 바다에 여행 가고 싶어요.
        그래서 여행지를 찾아요.

유진   마크 씨, 혹시 제주도에 가 봤어요?

마크   아니요, 아직 못 가 봤어요.

유진   그럼, 제주도에 가 보세요. 경치가 정말 좋아요.

마크   네, 제주도에 가 볼게요.
        그런데 제주도는 무슨 음식이 유명해요?

유진   해산물 요리가 유명해요.

마크   그래요? 정말 고마워요.

New Vocabulary

산 mountain
(이)나 or (between nouns)
바다 sea
여행가다 go on a trip
여행지 travel destination
찾다 find
아직 still
그런데 but, by the way
유명하다 famous
해산물 seafood

New Expressions

지금 뭐 해요?
What are you doing now?

혹시 제주도에 가 봤어요?
Have you ever been the Jeju Island?

아직 못 가 봤어요.
I have not been there yet.

경치가 정말 좋아요.
The view is really nice.

무슨 음식이 유명해요?
What food is famous?

Conversation Tips

★ **The marker (이)나**

The marker (이)나 is written between nouns and indicates choosing one noun between two options. If the noun before the marker ends in a vowel, 나 is used. If the noun ends with a consonant, 이나 is used.

커피나 차를 마셔요.	I drink coffee or tea.
밥이나 빵을 먹어요.	I eat rice or bread.

★ **그런데 "by the way, but"**

Use this when suddenly changing the topic.

고기 [고기] vs. 거기 [거기]

The vowels 'ㅗ' and 'ㅓ' are often mispronounced. Say 'ㅗ' with a rounded mouth, like the 'o' in "row." 'ㅓ' is pronounced like the 'a' in "awake." Practice the following.

(1) 도 (also) vs. 더 (more)

(2) 소리 (sound) vs. 서리 (frost)

(3) 놓아요 (Put it on) vs. 넣어요 (Put it in)

Additional Vocabulary

Track 154

① ② ③

④ ⑤ ⑥

⑦ ⑧ ⑨

1	바쁘다	to be busy
2	심심하다	to be bored
3	시원하다	to be refreshing
4	건강하다	to be healthy
5	멋있다	to be stylish
6	예쁘다	to be pretty
7	맛있다	to be tasty
8	맵다	to be spicy
9	짜다	to be salty

힘들다	to be tough, difficult (situation)
괜찮다	to be OK
복잡하다	to be complicated
간단하다	to be simple
아름답다	to be beautiful
편리하다	to be convenient
불편하다	to be uncomfortable, inconvenient
달다	to be sweet
친절하다	to be friendly

Replying to compliments

A	You speak Korean well.		A	You sing well.
B	No, I can't speak Korean well.		B	Just a bit.

Giving encouragement

A	Cheer up.		A	Don't worry, everything will be fine.
B	Thanks.		B	Thanks.

Grammar

▶ Complete the sentence using -고 싶다. (1~3)

1 너무 피곤해요. 좀 _____.
　　　　　　　　　　　쉬다

2 점심을 못 먹었어요. 배고파요. 밥을 _____.
　　　　　　　　　　　　　　　　　　　　먹다

3 한국 친구가 있어요. 그 친구하고 한국어로 _____.
　　　　　　　　　　　　　　　　　　　　　　　얘기하다

▶ Look at the picture and complete the conversation as shown in the example below. (4~5)

Ex.　A 한국에서 <u>운전해 봤어요</u>?
　　　　　　　　　운전하다
　　　B 아니요.
　　　A 재미있어요. 한번 <u>해 보세요</u>.
　　　B 네, 해 볼게요.

4　A 여름에 삼계탕을 (1) _____?
　　　　　　　　　　　　먹다
　　B 아니요.
　　A 맛있어요. 한번 (2) _____.
　　B 네, 먹어 볼게요.

5　A 한복을 (1) _____?
　　　　　　　　　입다
　　B 아니요.
　　A 멋있어요. 한번 (2) _____.
　　B 네, 입어 볼게요.

Listening

▶ Listen to the question and choose the correct answer. (6~7)

Track 156

6 ⓐ 네, 김치가 있어요.

ⓑ 아니요, 안 매워요.

ⓒ 네, 김치가 없어요.

ⓓ 아니요, 김치를 만들 수 없어요.

7 ⓐ 네, 시작해 볼게요.

ⓑ 네, 공부하고 싶어요.

ⓒ 아니요, 아직 안 배웠어요.

ⓓ 아니요, 한번 배워 보세요.

Reading

▶ Read and choose the correct answer. (8~9)

한국 노래를 좋아해요?

혹시 한국 노래를 들어 봤어요?
우리는 한국대학교 노래 동아리 학생이에요.
우리하고 같이 한국 노래를 불러요. 한국 친구도 만날 수 있어요.
그리고 한국 문화도 배울 수 있어요.

• 언제 월·수 저녁 6:00~8:00
• 어디 한국대학교 한국빌딩 5층
• 누가 외국 사람은 누구나

• 얼마 무료
• 어떻게 인터넷으로 연락해 주세요.
  www.koreansong.ac.kr

8 왜 광고 (advertisement)를 했어요?

ⓐ 인터넷을 배우고 싶어요.

ⓑ 한국 노래를 듣고 싶어요.

ⓒ 한국 문화를 배우고 싶어요.

ⓓ 노래 동아리를 소개하고 싶어요.

9 뭐가 맞아요?

ⓐ 돈이 필요해요.

ⓑ 일주일에 두 번 만나요.

ⓒ 전화로 연락할 수 있어요.

ⓓ 외국 사람은 올 수 없어요.

Answers p.280

A Word on Culture

Q Culture of affection

Some words are central, yet unique, to the ways of thinking in a particular society or culture. Such words are very hard to translate. In the United States, for instance, history has endowed words such as "liberty" and "equality" with special meaning and importance. In Korean, perhaps an even more important and difficult word to understand for the foreigner is the word 정 (affection, warmth, feeling, sentiment, love).

The concept of 정 is an essential part of how Koreans view and express their relationships. Tenderhearted, affectionate people are valued as having a lot of 정. People from the rural area will often offer a complete stranger a meal and a place to sleep, have a lot of 정.

Certain gestures indicate 정. When serving rice, for instance, a Korean will always serve at least two scoops of rice per bowl; any less and one is lacking in 정. This gesture of giving freely emphasizes generosity and feeling over the logic of calculating how much someone might really eat.

As always, the best way to get to understand how Koreans think is to interact with them and get to know some of them. You will probably hear them talk a lot about 정. And hopefully, they'll say you have a lot of it.

Chapter 19 그다음에 오른쪽으로 가세요.

- The grammar pattern for commands with -(으)세요
- Abbreviated questions
- The formal polite form -(스)ㅂ니다

The grammar pattern for commands with -(으)세요

Appendix p.266

-(으)세요 is used with verbs when making polite commands. To form negative commands, add -지 마세요 to the stem.

	ending in a vowel	ending in a consonant
positive	하세요. Do.	읽으세요. Read.
negative	하지 마세요. Don't do.	읽지 마세요. Don't read.

하루에 1시간 운동하세요.

Exercise for an hour per day.

약속을 잊어버리지 마세요.

Don't forget your appointment.

I wonder...

- **Irregular verbs**

  듣다 → 들으세요.
  Listen.

  듣지 마세요.
  Don't listen.

  만들다 → 만드세요.
  Make.

  만들지 마세요.
  Don't make.

Abbreviated questions

When you don't want to repeat some part of the conversation over and over again, simply leave the repeated part out and just add -요.

A 사거리에서 어디로 가요?   Where do we go from the intersection?

B 왼쪽으로 가세요.   Please go left.

A 그다음은요?   And after that?
　(= 그다음은 어디로 가요?)

광화문에 가 주세요.
Please go to Gwanghwamun.

네, 알겠습니다.
Yes, OK.

The formal polite form -(스)ㅂ니다

In formal situations, such as in company meetings or public presentations, rather than using the informal polite form -아/어요, use the formal polite form -(스)ㅂ니다. In order to make the tense present, the stem of a verb or adjective is combined with -ㅂ니다 when it ends as a vowel, and -습니다 when it ends with a consonant. When asking a question, 다 on the end turns into 까?.

	ending in a vowel	ending in a consonant
Sentence	합니다.	듣습니다.
Question	합니까?	듣습니까?

A   어디에서 회의를 합니까?   Where are we having the meeting?

B   2층 회의실에서 합니다.   We're having the meeting in the second-floor meeting room.

A   오늘 날씨가 어떻습니까?   How is the weather today?

B   날씨가 정말 좋습니다.   The weather is really nice.

The formal equivalent of -예요/이에요 and 아니에요 look like this:

-예요/이에요 → -입니다

아니에요 → 아닙니다

Irregular verbs
알다 → 압니다
살다 → 삽니다

A   고향이 밴쿠버입니까?   Is Vancouver your hometown?

B   아닙니다. 토론토입니다.   No, it isn't. Toronto is.

Track 157

Jane	Please take me to Gwang-hwamun.
taxi driver	Where in Gwanghwamun?
Jane	Please take me to the front of the Gwanghwamun post office.
taxi driver	Yes, OK.
	(They ride in the car for a while.)
Jane	Sir, please stop in front of that convenience store.
taxi driver	Yes, OK.
	(After stopping the car)
Jane	How much is it?
taxi driver	It's 7,500 won.

제인　　　광화문에 가 주세요.

택시 기사　광화문 어디요?

제인　　　광화문 우체국 앞에 가 주세요.

택시 기사　네, 알겠습니다.
　　　　　 (They ride in the car for a while.)

제인　　　아저씨, 저기 편의점 앞에서 세워 주세요.

택시 기사　네, 알겠습니다.
　　　　　 (After stopping the car)

제인　　　얼마예요?

택시 기사　7,500원이에요.

New Vocabulary

광화문 Gwanghwamun (area of Seoul)

우체국 post office

아저씨 casual expression for a man over thirty

편의점 convenience store

세우다 to stop

New Expressions

광화문에 가 주세요.
Please go to Gwanghwamun.

광화문 어디요?
Where in Gwanghwamun?

세워 주세요. Please stop.

Conversation Tips

★ **어디요? "Where"**
This is a short way to ask someone for more specific information.

광화문 <u>어디요?</u>　　　　Where in Gwanghwamun?
　(= 어디에 가요?)　　　(= Where are you going?)

★ <u>저기 편의점 앞에서</u> **"In front of that convenience store"**
　① 　 ② 　 ③　　　　　③ 　① 　　　 ②
After "here" or "there," describe the place you want to go.

저기 학교 앞에서　　　　In front of that school

Mark	Please go to Myeongdong.
taxi driver	Yes, OK.
	(They ride in the car for a while.)
Mark	Sir, go straight to the traffic light. After that go to the right.
taxi driver	Yes. And after that?
Mark	Stop here.
taxi driver	Yes, OK.
Mark	Here's the money. Thank you.
taxi driver	Thank you. Goodbye.

마크	명동에 가 주세요.
택시 기사	네, 알겠습니다.
	(They ride in the car for a while.)
마크	저기 신호등까지 직진하세요. 그다음에 오른쪽으로 가세요.
택시 기사	네. 그다음은요?
마크	여기에서 세워 주세요.
택시 기사	네, 알겠습니다.
마크	돈 여기요. 수고하세요.
택시 기사	감사합니다. 안녕히 가세요.

New Vocabulary

명동 Myeongdong (area of Seoul)

신호등 traffic light

까지 the marker in the meaning of "until, up to"

직진하다 to go straight

오른쪽 right side

으로 the marker for the direction in the meaning of "to"

돈 money

수고하다 to thank (someone)

New Expressions

저기 신호등까지 직진하세요.
Go straight to the traffic light.

오른쪽으로 가세요.
Go to the right.

그다음은요? And after that?

돈 여기요. Here's the money.

수고하세요. Thank you.

Use this form of "thank you" if you are a customer (for example, to a taxi driver, waiters, etc.)

* This phrase literally means "good job."

Conversation Tips

★ **Giving directions**

When you wish to go to the right or left at a specific place, instruct the driver by naming the place where he should turn, then 오른쪽 "right" or 왼쪽 "left" and the marker 으로. Here, this marker 으로 has the meaning "in the direction of."

사거리에서 오른쪽으로 가세요.	Go <u>to</u> the right at the intersection.
편의점에서 왼쪽으로 가세요.	Go <u>to</u> the left at the convenience store.

● 갔어요 [가써요] vs. 가세요 [가세요]

The following pairs of words have similar pronunciations and are two different forms of the same one. The words on the left show the past tense form of a verb while the following words on the right show the commanding form of the same verb. As you can see, these two words in a pair carry different meanings. After you have figured out the differences in pronouncing these words, why don't you try using them in a conversation?

(1) 샀어요 (I bought it) vs. 사세요 (Buy it)

(2) 탔어요 (I got on it) vs. 타세요 (Get on it)

(3) 배웠어요 (I learned it) vs. 배우세요 (Learn it)

Additional Vocabulary

Track 160

1	타다	to get on, ride
2	내리다	to get off
3	지나다	to pass by
4	건너다	to cross
5	사거리	four-way intersection
6	횡단보도	crosswalk
7	신호등	traffic light
8	모퉁이	corner
9	버스 정류장	bus stop
10	지하철역	subway station
11	육교	pedestrian bridge
12	다리	bridge

Track **161**

Expressions to use when giving directions

신호등에서
오른쪽으로
가세요.

A Please go right at the traffic light.

은행에서
왼쪽으로
가세요.

A Please go left at the bank.

신호등까지
직진하세요.

A Please drive straight to the traffic light.

약국 앞에서
세워 주세요.

A Please stop in front of the pharmacy.

Grammar

▶ Complete the sentence using -(으)세요 or -지 마세요 as shown in the example below. (1~2)

1

○ 매일 1시간 <u>운동하세요</u> .
운동하다

○ 많이 (1)_____ .
걷다

○ 채소를 많이 (2)_____ .
먹다

2

✗ 너무 많이 <u>일하지 마세요</u> .
일하다

✗ 술을 많이 (1)_____ .
마시다

✗ 담배를 (2)_____ .
피우다

▶ Complete the paragraph using -(스)ㅂ니다 as shown in the example below.

3

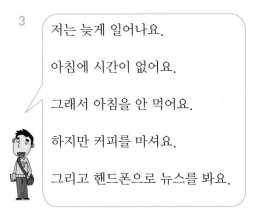

저는 늦게 일어나요.

아침에 시간이 없어요.

그래서 아침을 안 먹어요.

하지만 커피를 마셔요.

그리고 핸드폰으로 뉴스를 봐요.

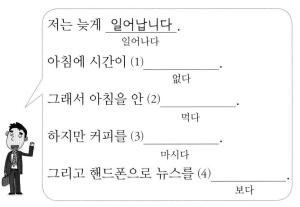

저는 늦게 <u>일어납니다</u> .
일어나다

아침에 시간이 (1)_____ .
없다

그래서 아침을 안 (2)_____ .
먹다

하지만 커피를 (3)_____ .
마시다

그리고 핸드폰으로 뉴스를 (4)_____ .
보다

▶ Choose the correct answer to complete the conversation. (4~5)

4   A 어디로 가요?

     B 저기 은행에서 오른쪽으로 가세요.

     A (ⓐ 그다음은요? / ⓑ 어디로 가요?)

     B 왼쪽으로 가세요.

5   A 마크 씨, 몇 시에 집에 가요?

     B 보통 7시에 집에 가요. (ⓐ 몇 시요? / ⓑ 제인 씨는요?)

     A 저는 3시에 집에 가요.

▶ Listen and choose the correct answer. (6~7)

Track 162

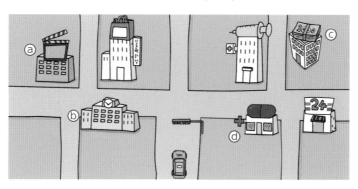

6 여자가 어디에서 내려요? (   )

7 뭐가 맞아요?

　　ⓐ 여자가 길을 몰라요.　　　　　　ⓑ 택시비가 7,400원이에요.

　　ⓒ 여자가 택시를 탈 거예요.　　　　ⓓ 여자가 버스로 명동에 가요.

Reading

▶ Read and choose the correct answer. (8~9)

> 제인은 운동을 정말 좋아합니다. 특히 스키와 수영을 좋아합니다.
> (　　) 제인은 겨울마다 스키 타러 산에 갑니다. 그리고 여름에는 수영하러 바다에 갑니다.
> 봄과 가을에는 날씨가 좋습니다. 그래서 공원에서 책을 읽습니다.

8 (　　)에 알맞은 답을 고르세요.

　　ⓐ 그리고　　　　　ⓑ 그런데　　　　　ⓒ 그래서　　　　　ⓓ 왜냐하면

9 뭐가 맞아요?

　　ⓐ 제인은 스키를 탈 수 있습니다.　　　ⓑ 제인은 수영을 할 수 없습니다.

　　ⓒ 제인은 수영하러 수영장에 갑니다.　　ⓓ 여름하고 겨울에 공원에서 책을 읽습니다.

Answers p.280 and p.281

A Word on Culture

Q When do I need to use formal language?

One of the most difficult aspects of learning Korean is understanding what degree of formality is appropriate for each occasion. Because Korean culture is based on hierarchical relationships between people, some understanding of this part of Korean culture is essential to learning to speak the language well.

So when do you use formal language? If you were to get dressed up and go in front of an audience to make a speech in Korean, or to get in front of the camera to give the news, you would use formal language -(스)ㅂ니다 without hesitation. Formal language excludes the feeling of intimacy, and though it feels somewhat stiff, formal language is considered appropriate for formal occasions.

On the other hand, -아/어요 is used to establish a more relaxed atmosphere. With people you meet every day and with whom you feel you have a close relationship, such as your neighbor or store owners, you may use -아/어요. However, there must be a mutual familiarity.

People working in service industries – such as salespeople at department stores or agents at an airport – usually use formal language -(스)ㅂ니다, although if they wish to come across in a more friendly way, they might use -아/어요.

As it is with clothes, language should suit the occasion. So when you are thinking about approaching someone, decide whether you should use formal language -(스)ㅂ니다 or –아/어요 before speaking.

Chapter 20

성함이 어떻게 되세요?

- Honorific language for the subject of a sentence
- Honorific language for the listener

몇 분이세요?
How many people are there?

4명이요.
Four people.

● ## Honorific language for the subject of a sentence

Appendix p.266

English speakers often confuse formal language and honorific language. Remember this: the situation will govern the decision to use formal or informal language; the subject of the sentence determines whether to use honorific language or not.

The honorific for the subject of a sentence in an informal situation

Use honorific language when the subject of the sentence is someone older than yourself, such as your grandmother, grandfather, father, or mother. In an honorific sentence, the subject marker 이/가 is replaced by the marker 께서 and the present tense verb ending becomes -(으)세요, the past tense verb ending becomes -(으)셨어요, and the future tense verb ending becomes -(으)실 거예요.

	ending in a vowel	ending in a consonant
present	하세요.	읽으세요.
past	하셨어요.	읽으셨어요.
future	하실 거예요.	읽으실 거예요.

1 normal 진수가 운동해요.   Jinsu exercises.

  honorific 할아버지께서 운동하세요.   Grandfather exercises.

2 normal 동생이 음악을 들었어요.   My younger brother listened to music.

  honorific 어머니께서 음악을 들으셨어요.   My mother listened to music.

3 normal 친구가 이따가 올 거예요.   My friend will come later.

  honorific 아버지께서 이따가 오실 거예요.   My father will come later.

성함이 어떻게 **되세요?**
What is your name?

마크 피터스**입니다.**
I'm Mark Peters.

Honorific language for the listener

When you are asking a question to someone older, a stranger, or someone to whom you need to show respect, use honorific language. In your conversations with Koreans, you have probably been on the receiving end of many of these honorific questions. But remember, when you answer the questions, don't use honorific language (because you're talking about yourself)!

1   A   어디에 가세요?   Where are you going?

    B   회사에 가요.   I'm going to the office.

2   A   뉴스 보셨어요?   Did you see the news?

    B   아니요, 못 봤어요.   No, I didn't see it.

The honorific for the listener in a formal situation

The last chapter briefly introduced the formal polite form -(스)ㅂ니다. In everyday life, the informal honorific -(으)세요 is most widely used. However, you will often hear formal language, even if you don't use it much yourself. In settings where Koreans use formal language (such as when making a speech, when talking to a customer, etc.), they often use honorific language as well, since they are often speaking to strangers or someone to whom they need to show respect. Formal honorific statements end in -(으)십니다 and formal honorific questions end in -(으)십니까. For instance, an informal honorific greeting is "안녕하세요"; but "안녕하십니까" is a formal honorific greeting. Note the different endings.

    A   일을 다 끝내셨습니까?   Have you finished your work?

    B   네, 끝냈습니다.   Yes, I've finished it.

Track **163**

오늘 저녁 6시에 예약돼요?

네, 됩니다.

Paul	Is it possible to make a reservation for dinner tonight at 6?
staff	Yes, it's possible. How many people will come?
Paul	Four people.
staff	May I have your name?
Paul	My name is Paul Smith.
staff	Please give me your phone number.
Paul	It is 010-2798-3541.
staff	Great, your reservation is set.

폴   오늘 저녁 6시에 예약돼요?

직원   네, 됩니다. 몇 분 오실 거예요?

폴   4명요.

직원   성함이 어떻게 되세요?

폴   제 이름은 폴 스미스입니다.

직원   연락처를 가르쳐 주세요.

폴   010-2798-3541이에요.

직원   네, 예약됐습니다.

New Vocabulary

예약 reservation

되다 to be possible, available

분 counting word for people 〔honorific〕

몇 분 how many people 〔honorific〕

성함 name 〔honorific〕

연락처 contact information (phone number)

New Expressions

예약돼요? Is it possible to make a reservation?

네, 됩니다. Yes, it's possible.

몇 분 오실 거예요? How many people will come?

성함이 어떻게 되세요? May I have your name? 〔honorific〕

연락처를 가르쳐 주세요. Please tell me your contact information.

예약됐습니다. Your reservation is set.

Conversation Tips

★ **성함이 어떻게 되세요?** "May I have your name?"

This is the honorific way of asking someone's name. As an adult, you will most often use this to ask someone's name (though you might use "이름이 뭐예요?" to someone much younger). You will often hear it in hotels and other places where people meet for the first time. Do not use this honorific language on yourself!

★ **When introducing oneself, speak formally**

Koreans tend to use -입니다 rather than -예요/이에요 when giving their full names during an introduction, making a reservation, etc.

며칠 동안
묵으실 거예요?

3일 동안

Jane	I want to make a reservation for a room for next weekend.
concierge	How many days will you be staying?
Jane	I'll be staying for three days starting on Friday. Do you have a double room?
concierge	Yes, we have one. May I have your name?
Jane	Jane Brown.
concierge	Please come by 6 on Friday.
Jane	Yes, got it.

제인   다음 주말에 방을 예약하고 싶어요.

직원   며칠 동안 묵으실 거예요?

제인   금요일부터 3일 동안 묵을 거예요.
2인실 있어요?

직원   네, 있습니다. 성함이 어떻게 되세요?

제인   제인 브라운입니다.

직원   금요일 저녁 6시까지 와 주세요.

제인   네, 알겠습니다.

New Vocabulary

주말 weekend
다음 주말에 next weekend
방 room
예약하다 to make a reservation
며칠 동안 how many days
묵다 to stay, lodge
2인실 double room
까지 by (a time)

New Expressions

며칠 동안 묵으실 거예요?
How many days are you staying?

금요일부터 3일 동안 묵을 거예요.
I'll be staying for three days starting on Friday.

2인실 있어요?
Do you have a double room?

6시까지 와 주세요.
Please come by 6.

Conversation Tips

★ **얼마 동안 = 며칠 동안 "how many days"**
These two expressions have the same meaning, but a slightly different nuance. A question with 며칠 동안 really asks for a specific number of days while 얼마 동안 could be answered with a different unit of time (year, month, day, hour, etc.).

★ **For one person**
In hotels, a room for one person is called 1 (일) 인실, and in restaurants, a portion of food for one person is called 1 (일) 인분.

★ **The marker 까지 "by"**
Using the marker 까지 after a unit of time conveys a time limit.
내일 1시까지 오세요. Come by 1 tomorrow.

● 연락처 [열락처]

When 'ㄴ' occurs immediately before or after 'ㄹ', 'ㄴ' is pronounced as [ㄹ].

(1) ㄴ → [ㄹ] 관리 [괄리], 신라 [실라]

(2) ㄴ → [ㄹ] 설날 [설랄], 한글날 [한글랄]

Additional Vocabulary

Track 166

기분이 좋다
to feel good

기분이 나쁘다
to feel bad

놀라다
to feel surprised

아프다
to feel sick

행복하다
to feel happy

슬프다
to feel sad

당황하다
to feel embarrassed
(because of an unexpected action)

졸리다
to feel sleepy

화가 나다
to feel angry

무섭다
to feel afraid

피곤하다
to feel tired

부끄럽다
to feel bashful

Useful Phrases

Track 167

Payment

A May I pay by credit card?
B I'm sorry, sir. We don't accept credit cards.
When you want to know if it's possible to use a credit card.

A How should I do this for you?
B Please charge it in one lump sum.
When using a credit card.

※ When you want to make several payments:
　3개월 할부로 해 주세요.
　"Please divide it into 3 monthly installments."

※ When a salesman asks for your signature:
　여기에 사인해 주세요. "Please sign here."

Delivery

A Mister, do you deliver?
B Of course, we do.
When you want to know if a delivery is possible.

A Please deliver one pizza.
B Yes, got it.
When ordering delivery over the phone.

Grammar

▶ Complete the paragraph using the honorific language as shown in the example below.

1

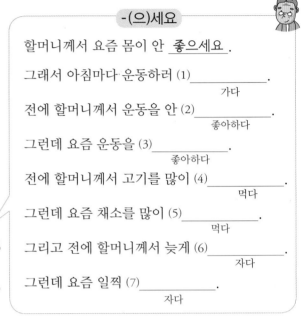

-아/어요

친구가 요즘 몸이 안 좋아요.

그래서 아침마다 운동하러 가요.

전에 친구가 운동을 안 좋아했어요.

그런데 요즘 운동을 좋아해요.

전에 친구가 고기를 많이 먹었어요.

그런데 요즘 채소를 많이 먹어요.

그리고 전에 친구가 늦게 잤어요.

그런데 요즘 일찍 자요.

-(으)세요

할머니께서 요즘 몸이 안 <u>좋으세요</u>.

그래서 아침마다 운동하러 (1)_____.
　　　　　　　　　　　　　　　　가다

전에 할머니께서 운동을 안 (2)_____.
　　　　　　　　　　　　　　　좋아하다

그런데 요즘 운동을 (3)_____.
　　　　　　　　　　　좋아하다

전에 할머니께서 고기를 많이 (4)_____.
　　　　　　　　　　　　　　　　먹다

그런데 요즘 채소를 많이 (5)_____.
　　　　　　　　　　　　　먹다

그리고 전에 할머니께서 늦게 (6)_____.
　　　　　　　　　　　　　　　　자다

그런데 요즘 일찍 (7)_____.
　　　　　　　　　　자다

▶ Choose the best answer. (2~3)

2　(1) 저는 친구 (ⓐ 이름 / ⓑ 성함)을 몰라요.

　　(2) 저는 선생님 (ⓐ 이름 / ⓑ 성함)을 몰라요.

3　(1) 저는 친구 (ⓐ 나이 / ⓑ 연세)를 알아요.

　　(2) 저는 할아버지 (ⓐ 나이 / ⓑ 연세)를 알아요.

▶ Complete the conversation using the honorific language as shown in the example below. (4~6)

Ex.　A　한국 생활은 재미있으세요?

　　　B　네, 재미있어요.

4　A　한국어를 _____?

　　B　네, 배워요.

5　A　한국어 공부가 _____?

　　B　네, 좀 어려워요.

6　A　어제 무슨 음식을 _____?

　　B　불고기를 먹었어요.

▶ Listen and choose the correct answer. (7~8)

Track 168

7 왜 제인이 전화했어요?

    ⓐ 식당 길을 알고 싶어요.   ⓑ 식당을 예약하고 싶어요.

    ⓒ 식당 시간을 알고 싶어요.   ⓓ 식당 전화번호를 알고 싶어요.

8 뭐가 맞아요?

    ⓐ 이 식당은 전화 예약이 안 돼요.   ⓑ 제인은 식당 전화번호를 몰라요.

    ⓒ 제인은 8시까지 식당에 갈 거예요.   ⓓ 제인은 다른 사람 두 명하고 같이 갈 거예요.

Reading

▶ Read and choose the correct answer.

9 뭐가 맞아요?

    ⓐ 호텔이 산 옆에 있습니다.

    ⓑ 전화로 예약할 수 없습니다.

    ⓒ 전화 예약은 5% 할인됩니다.

    ⓓ 인터넷 예약이 15% 할인됩니다.

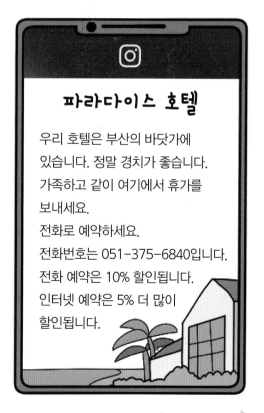

파라다이스 호텔

우리 호텔은 부산의 바닷가에 있습니다. 정말 경치가 좋습니다. 가족하고 같이 여기에서 휴가를 보내세요.
전화로 예약하세요.
전화번호는 051-375-6840입니다.
전화 예약은 10% 할인됩니다.
인터넷 예약은 5% 더 많이 할인됩니다.

Answers p.281

A Word on Culture

미역국 Seaweed soup

삼계탕
Ginseng chicken soup

팥죽 Red bean porridge

Q Do you know what foods Koreans eat on special days?

Walking down the street on a humid summer day, you may come upon long lines of Koreans in front of a restaurant. That restaurant is probably a 삼계탕 (chicken boiled with ginseng) restaurant. It may seem strange, but Koreans believe that drinking hot soup on a hot day restores one's energy and vitality. This thinking comes from Chinese medicine. Thus, on the hottest days of the year, most Koreans eat 삼계탕.

On birthdays, whether spent with friends at a party or quietly in one's own home, Koreans without exception eat 미역국 (seaweed soup). Traditionally, this soup is eaten by mothers who have just gone through childbirth in order to thank the god of childbirth for a healthy baby. These days, the practice is continued, not to thank the gods, but for the sake of the mother. Seaweed has many nutrients which aid in recovery after childbirth, so most women drink this soup several times a day for a month or so. Thus, Koreans continue to drink this soup on their birthdays and think of their mothers.

On the winter solstice, Koreans eat 팥죽, a type of congee made from red beans. In ancient times, people considered this the first day of a new year and believed that eating 팥죽 would cleanse the body of bad spirits. The color of this congee was thought to scare the bad spirits away.

How do you feel about trying these foods?

APPENDIX

Extra Grammar Tips

Grammar Review

Answers

Glossary of Words

Extra Grammar Tips

Chap. 5 Counting words p.105

	개	명	분	마리	잔	권	장
one	한 개	한 명	한 분	한 마리	한 잔	한 권	한 장
two	두 개	두 명	두 분	두 마리	두 잔	두 권	두 장
three	세 개	세 명	세 분	세 마리	세 잔	세 권	세 장
four	네 개	네 명	네 분	네 마리	네 잔	네 권	네 장
five	다섯 개	다섯 명	다섯 분	다섯 마리	다섯 잔	다섯 권	다섯 장
twenty	스무 개	스무 명	스무 분	스무 마리	스무 잔	스무 권	스무 장
twenty-one	스물한 개	스물한 명	스물한 분	스물한 마리	스물한 잔	스물한 권	스물한 장
many	여러 개	여러 명	여러 분	여러 마리	여러 잔	여러 권	여러 장

Chap. 7 The structure of questions with "be" verbs p.124

집이 **어디**예요?	**Where** is your house?
생일이 **언제**예요?	**When** is your birthday?
이름이 **뭐**예요?	**What** is your name?
저분이 **누구**예요?	**Who** is that person?

몇 시…?	What time …?
A 회의가 **몇 시**예요?	A **What time** is the meeting?
B 1시 20분이에요. (한 시 이십 분이에요.)	B It is at 1:20.
몇 번…?	What number …?
A 전화번호가 **몇 번**이에요?	A **What** is your phone **number**?
B 9326-7435예요. (구삼이육에 칠사삼오예요.)	B It is a 326-7435.
몇 명…?	How many people …?
A 가족이 **몇 명**이에요?	A **How many people** are in your family?
B 5명이에요. (다섯 명이에요.)	B Five people.

1. 해요	2. -아요	3. -어요
	If the last syllable of the stem has a '하' or '工' vowel, add -아요 to the stem. **받다 → 받아요** (받 + -아요 → 받아요) 살다 → 살아요 놀다 → 놀아요	If the last syllable of the stem has a '하', '一' or 'I' vowel, add -어요 to the stem. **먹다 → 먹어요** (먹 + -어요 → 먹어요) 읽다 → 읽어요 찍다 → 찍어요
If the 하다 verb is changed to the present tense, it always becomes 해요. **공부하다 → 공부해요** 일하다　　→ 일해요 운전하다 → 운전해요 시작하다 → 시작해요 여행하다 → 여행해요 준비하다 → 준비해요 연습하다 → 연습해요 말하다　　→ 말해요	If there are two '하' vowels in a row, one is dropped. **가다 → 가요** (가 + -아요 → 가요) 만나다 → 만나요 끝나다 → 끝나요	If the vowels '하' and '하' occur together, '하' is dropped. **보내다 → 보내요** (보내 + -어요 → 보내요) 지내다 → 지내요
	If the verb stem ends in the vowel '工', '工' and '하' combine to form '와'. **오다 → 와요** (오 + -아요 → 와요) 보다 → 봐요	If the verb stem ends in the vowel '一', '一' and '하' combine to form '하'. **주다 → 줘요** (주 + -어요 → 줘요) 배우다 → 배워요
		If the stem ends in the vowel 'I', it becomes '하'. **마시다 → 마셔요** (마시 + -어요 → 마셔요) 가르치다 → 가르쳐요 기다리다 → 기다려요

그리고 "and"	날씨가 좋아요. **그리고** 사람들이 친절해요. The weather is good. **And** the people are friendly.
그런데, 하지만 "but"	한국어 공부가 재미있어요. **그런데** 좀 어려워요. Studying Korean is interesting. **But** it's a bit difficult.
그래서 "so, therefore"	배가 아파요. **그래서** 병원에 가요. My stomach hurts. **So**, I'm going to the hospital.
그러니까 "so, therefore"	비가 와요. **그러니까** 우산을 가지고 가세요. It is raining. **So**, take an umbrella with you.
그러면 (= 그럼) "then, so"	한국어를 잘하고 싶어요? **그러면** 한국 친구하고 많이 얘기해요. Do you want to be good at Korean? (**If so**,) Have a lot of conversations with Korean friends.

Verb	Form	Commands with -(으)세요	Honorific language		
			Present -(으)세요	Past -(으)셨어요	Future -(으)실 거예요
먹다, 마시다	드시다	드세요	드세요	드셨어요	드실 거예요
있다	계시다	계세요	계세요	계셨어요	계실 거예요
자다	주무시다	주무세요	주무세요	주무셨어요	주무실 거예요

The verb examples above are changed to special forms (Ex. 먹다 → 드시다) when used for honorific purposes.

	Non-honorific (normal)	Honorific
Name	이름 이름이 뭐예요?	성함 성함이 어떻게 되세요?
Age	나이 나이가 몇 살이에요?	연세 연세가 어떻게 되세요?
House	집 집이 어디예요?	댁 댁이 어디세요?
Meal	밥 밥 먹었어요?	진지 진지 드셨어요?

Most of the time, the only difference between honorific language and regular language is the verb. But in some cases, nouns also change into their honorific equivalents.

Grammar Review

▶ THESE ARE COMMONLY CONFUSED ◀

1 How to read numbers   chap. 5 and 6

Native Korean numbers	Sino-Korean Numbers
Counting 가방 1개 (한 개) one bag 친구 2명 (두 명) two friends 커피 3잔 (세 잔) three cups of coffee	**Reading Numbers** Numbers 1번 (일 번) Phone numbers 7019–8423 (칠공일구에 팔사이삼) Dates 2016년 3월 9일 (이천십육 년 삼 월 구 일) Prices 24,500원 (이만 사천오백 원) Addresses 서울 아파트 102동 (백이 동) 603호 (육백삼 호) Building floors 5층 (오 층)
Age 15살 (열다섯 살) 15 years old	
Time, Hours 5시 (다섯 시)예요. It is five o'clock. 2시간 (두 시간) 일했어요. I worked for two hours.	**Minutes** 5분 (오 분)이에요. It is five minutes.
Month 1달 (한 달) 동안 여행했어요. I traveled for a month.	**Year, Week, Day** 1년 (일 년) 동안 살았어요. I lived there for a year. 2주일 (이 주일) 동안 준비했어요. I prepared for two weeks. 3일 (삼 일) 동안 전화 안 했어요. I didn't call for three days.

2 -예요/이에요 vs. 있어요   chap.1,4, and 6

-예요/이에요	있어요
When there is a correspondence between the subject and something else.	When expressing the existence of something in a particular time or place.
마크가 폴 친구예요. Mark **is** Paul's friende. 선생님이 한국 사람이에요. The teacher **is** Korean.	제니가 집에 **있어요**. Jenny **is** at home. 학생이 학교에 **있어요**. The student **is** at school.

아니에요	없어요
When a correspondence doesn't exist; the opposite of -예요/이에요.	When something doesn't exist in a particular time or place; the opposite of 있어요.
제니는 남자가 **아니에요**. Jenny **is not** a man. 폴은 미국 사람이 **아니에요**. Paul **is not** American.	제임스가 집에 **없어요**. James **is not** at home.

3 from … to … chap.8, 9, and 12

place ···에서 ···까지	서울에서 부산까지 버스로 4시간 걸려요. It takes 4 hours **from** Seoul **to** Busan by bus.
time ···부터 ···까지	1시부터 3시까지 공부해요. I study **from** 1 o'clock **to** 3 o'clock.
person ···한테서 ···한테	친구한테서 얘기 들었어요. 하지만 다른 친구한테 말 안 할 거예요. I heard that story **from** my friend. But I won't tell it **to** my other friend.

4 시 vs. 시간 chap.8 and 9

time 시	2시에 친구를 만나요. I meet my friend at **two o'clock**.
time duration 시간	2시간 동안 영화를 봤어요. I watched the movie for **two hours**.

5 이, 그, 저 chap.3

	이 ("this")	그 ("that")	저 ("that")
When to use	When the object being referred to is close to the speaker.	1) When the object being referred to is close to the listener. 2) When the object being referred to is not visible to both speaker and listener.	When the object being referred to is visible but far from both speaker and listener.
When modifying a noun	이 사람 this person	그 사람 that person	저 사람 that person
이것, 저것, 그것 + subject marker 이	이게 this thing (with subject marker 이)	그게 that thing (with subject marker 이)	저게 that thing (with subject marker 이)
이것, 저것, 그것 + marker 은	이건 this thing (with marker 은)	그건 that thing (with marker 은)	저건 that thing (with marker 은)
Adverb	여기 here	거기 there	저기 there

▶ IRREGULAR VERBS ◀

① ㄷ irregular verbs p. 174

When a stem ends in 'ㄷ', this 'ㄷ' becomes 'ㄹ' whenever the ending begins with a vowel (such as the present tense -아/어요).

듣다 → 듣 + -어요 → 들 + -어요 → 들어요

한국 음악을 자주 들어요. I often listen to Korean music.

② ㅂ irregular verbs p. 184

When a stem ends in 'ㅂ', this 'ㅂ' becomes 우 whenever the ending begins with a vowel (such as the present tense -아/어요). Then combine the 우 with the ending -어요 to form the ending -워요.

쉽다 → 쉽 + -어요 → 쉬우 + -어요 → 쉬워요

한국어가 쉬워요. Korean is easy.

③ 으 irregular verbs p. 184

When the stem ends with the vowel 으, this 으 is dropped whenever the ending begins with a vowel (such as the present tense -아/어요).

바쁘다 → 바쁘 + -아요 → 바ㅃ + -아요 → 바빠요

인호가 정말 바빠요. Inho is really busy.

④ ㄹ irregular verbs p. 245

When a verb stem ends in 'ㄹ', this 'ㄹ' is dropped whenever the consonants such as 'ㄴ', 'ㅂ', and 'ㅅ' come next.

살다 → 살 + -ㅂ니다 → 사 + -ㅂ니다 → 삽니다

저는 한국에서 삽니다. I live in Korea.

⑤ 르 irregular verbs p. 184

When a verb stem ends in 르, before -아/어요 the 'ㅡ' is dropped and one more 'ㄹ' is added to the syllable preceding the original 'ㄹ'.

다르다 → 다르 + -아요 → 달ㄹ + -아요 → 달라요

한국어는 영어하고 너무 달라요. Korean is too different from English.

▶ MARKERS ◀

1 The subject marker 이/가

ending in a vowel	ending in a consonant
폴 씨가 호주 사람이에요.	선생님이 한국 사람이에요.
Paul is Australian.	The teacher is Korean.

2 The object marker 을/를

ending in a vowel	ending in a consonant
커피를 좋아해요.	물을 마셔요.
I like coffee.	I drink water.

3 The marker 은/는

ending in a vowel	ending in a consonant
저는 폴이에요.	선생님은 한국 사람이에요.
I am Paul.	The teacher is Korean.

(1) Topic marker: Indicating emphasis with a gesture.

저는 마크예요. 그리고 저분은 제 선생님이에요.

I am Mark, and that person is my teacher.

(2) To stress contrast.

비빔밥은 좋아해요. 그런데 김치는 안 좋아해요.

I like Bibimbap, but I don't like Kimchi.

(3) Placed after something you wish to stress.

A 머리가 아파요.   My head hurts.

B 약은 먹었어요?   Did you take some medicine?

4 The time marker 에

It doesn't matter whether the time ends in a vowel or consonant.

3시에 만나요.   Let's meet at 3:00.

6시 30분에 끝나요.   It ends at 6:30 (six-thirty).

Marker 에: Use this marker with verbs 가다/오다.
학교에 가요. I go to school.

(1) Place marker 에: Use this place marker with verbs 있다/없다.
집에 있어요. I am at home.
(2) Place marker 에서: Use this place marker with all other action verbs.
집에서 일해요. I work at home.

(1) 한테 to (somebody)
폴이 부모님한테 이메일을 보내요. Paul sends an email to his parents.
(2) 한테서 from (somebody)
앤이 친구한테서 선물을 받았어요. Ann received a present from a friend.
(3) 에서 from (place)
마크가 미국에서 왔어요. Mark came from the U.S.
(4) ···에서 ···까지 from ··· to ···(place)
집에서 회사까지 시간이 얼마나 걸려요?
How long does it take to go from home to the office?
(5) ···부터 ···까지 from ··· to ···(time)
1시부터 2시까지 점심시간이에요. Lunch time is from 1 to 2 o'clock.
(6) 까지 until
어제 새벽 2시까지 공부했어요. Yesterday I studied until 2 in the morning.
(7) 도 also
저도 영화를 좋아해요. I also like movies.
(8) 만 only
제 동생은 고기만 먹어요. My younger brother eats only meat.
(9) 마다 every
일요일마다 친구를 만나요. I meet friends every Sunday.
(10) (으)로 by means of
매일 학교에 지하철로 가요. I go to school by subway everyday.
(11) (으)로 by
사람들은 젓가락으로 국수를 먹어요. People eat noodles by using chopsticks.
(12) (으)로 toward, to
남쪽으로 가세요. Go to the south.

▶ QUESTION WORDS ◀

Person

▶ 누가 who
Used when "who" is the subject of the sentence. Used with the subject marker 가.
누가 사무실에 있어요?   Who is in the office?
누가 운동해요?   Who is exercising?

▶ 누구
(1) **who**: Used together with -예요.
이분이 누구예요?   Who is this person?

(2) **whom**
- Used with the object marker 를.
누구를 좋아해요?   Whom do you like?
- Used with the marker 하고 (with).
누구하고 식사해요?   With whom do you eat?
- Used with the marker 한테 (to).
누구한테 전화해요?   To whom are you calling?
- Used with the marker 한테서 (from).
누구한테서 한국어를 배워요?   From whom do you learn Korean?

(3) **whose**: Used for possession.
이 가방이 누구 거예요?   Whose bag is this?

Things

▶ 뭐 what
(1) Used with -예요.
이름이 뭐예요?   What is your name?

(2) Used with other verbs.
오늘 오후에 뭐 해요?   What are you doing this afternoon?

▶ 무슨 what kind of
Used when asking about the content or attributes of something.
무슨 영화를 좋아해요?   What kind of movies do you like?

▶ 어느 which
Used when choosing among a range of possibilities.
어느 나라 사람이에요?   Which nationality are you?

272 · Korean made easy for beginners (2nd edition)

▶ 어떤 what/which

(1) Used when asking about attributes or features.

어떤 음식을 좋아해요? What kind of food do you like?

(2) Used when choosing among a range of possibilities.

이 중에서 어떤 옷을 사고 싶어요? Which clothes do you want to buy?

▶ 몇

(1) how many

■ Used with the counting word 개 for things.

가방이 몇 개 있어요? How many bags are there?

■ Used with the counting word 명 for people.

사람이 몇 명 있어요? How many people are there?

■ Used with the counting word 번 for time frequency.

제주도에 몇 번 가 봤어요? How many times have you been to Jeju Island?

(2) what

■ Used when reading a number.

전화번호가 몇 번이에요? What is your phone number?

■ Used when reading time.

몇 시 몇 분이에요? What time is it? (asking specific hours and minutes of the time)

③ **Time**

▶ 언제 when

(1) Used with -예요.

생일이 언제예요? When is your birthday?

(2) Used with other verbs (note that the time marker 에 is unnecessary).

언제 파티에 가요? When are you going to the party?

▶ 며칠 what day

(1) Used with -이에요.

오늘이 며칠이에요? What day is today?

(2) Used with other verbs (the time marker 에 is needed).

며칠에 가요? On what day are you going?

▶ **몇 시 what time**

(1) Used with -예요.

지금 몇 시예요? What time is it now?

(2) Used with other verbs (the time marker 에 is needed).

몇 시에 **운동해요**? What time do you exercise?

▶ **무슨 요일 what day of week**

(1) Used with -이에요.

오늘이 무슨 요일이에요? What day of the week is today?

(2) Used with other verbs (the time marker 에 is needed).

무슨 요일에 **영화를 봐요**? What day of the week do you watch movies?

---

4 Place

▶ **어디 where**

(1) Used with -예요.

집이 어디예요? Where is your house?

(2) Used with verbs 가다/오다 (the marker 에 is needed.)

어디에 **가요**? Where are you going?

(3) Used with verbs 있다/없다 (the place marker 에 is needed).

화장실이 어디에 **있어요**? Where is the restroom?

(4) Used with other action verbs (the place marker 에서 is needed).

어디에서 **친구를 만나요**? Where are you meeting your friend?

---

5 Others

▶ **얼마 how much**: Used with -예요.

이게 얼마예요? How much is this?

▶ **얼마나 how long / how much time**: Used with the verb 걸려요.

시간이 얼마나 **걸려요**? How much time does it take?

▶ **얼마 동안 how long**: Used with other verbs.

얼마 동안 **한국에 살았어요**? How long have you lived in Korea?

▶ **어떻게 how**: Used when asking about a means of doing something.

어떻게 **집에 가요**? How do you go home?

▶ **왜 why**: Used when asking about a reason for something.

왜 **한국어를 공부해요**? Why are you studying Korean?

Answers

Hangeul 1 — p.24

1 X   2 O   3 X   4 ⓑ
5 ⓓ   6 ⓐ   7 ⓒ   8 ⓐ
9 ⓑ   10 ⓑ
11 나이   12 소
13 가수   14 나무

Hangeul 2 — p.34

1 ⓑ   2 ⓐ   3 ⓑ   4 ⓐ
5 ⓑ   6 ⓑ   7 ⓑ   8 ⓐ
9 ⓑ   10 ⓐ   11 ⓒ   12 ⓑ
13 ⓓ   14 ⓑ
15 요리   16 여유
17 다리   18 바지
19 물건   20 한국

Hangeul 3 — p.44

1 ⓑ   2 ⓐ   3 ⓑ   4 ⓑ
5 ⓐ   6 ⓑ   7 ⓒ   8 ⓒ
9 ⓑ   10 ⓓ   11 ⓑ   12 ⓐ
13 ⓓ
14 세금   15 계란
16 카메라   17 컴퓨터
18 옆   19 윷

Hangeul 4 — p.54

1 ⓒ   2 ⓑ   3 ⓐ   4 ⓑ
5 ⓐ   6 ⓓ   7 ⓒ   8 ⓓ
9 ⓑ   10 ⓑ
11 의지   12 사과
13 오빠   14 딸기
15 벚꽃   16 찜닭

Chapter 1 — p.70

▶ **Grammar**

1 예요   2 예요
3 이에요   4 한국
5 일본 사람이에요   6 저는 미국 사람이에요
7 뭐   8 어느 나라

▶ **Listening**

9 A 이름이 뭐예요?
  B 제임스예요.
  A 어느 나라 사람이에요?
  B 영국 사람이에요.

Track 046

10 A 이름이 뭐예요?
   B 인호예요.
   A 어느 나라 사람이에요?
   B 한국 사람이에요.

11 A 이름이 뭐예요?
   B 유웨이예요.
   A 어느 나라 사람이에요?
   B 중국 사람이에요.

9 ⓒ, ㉮   10 ⓑ, ㉰
11 ⓐ, ㉯

► **Reading**

12 ⓓ

Chapter 2   p.80

► **Grammar**

1 네, 아니요   2 아니요, 네

3 영어   4 한국어

5 ⓒ   6 ⓐ   7 ⓑ

► **Listening**

8   A 제인 씨, 회사원이에요?
    B 아니요.
    A 그럼, 의사예요?
    B 아니요.
    A 그럼, 학생이에요?
    B 아니요.
    A 그럼, 선생님이에요?
    B 네, 맞아요.

Track 052

9   A 민호 씨, 학생이에요?
    B 아니요.
    A 그럼, 무슨 일 해요?
    B 선생님이에요.
    A 그럼, 한국어 선생님이에요?
    B 아니요, 일본어 선생님이에요.

8 ⓐ   9 ⓓ

► **Reading**

10 (1) ⓑ   (2) ⓐ

Chapter 3   p.90

► **Grammar**

1 이   2 가   3 이   4 가

5 마크   6 제인 씨예요

7 (1) 시계예요   (2) 유진 씨

8 (1) 이게   (2) 누구

► **Listening**

9   ⓐ 시계예요.   ⓑ 의자예요.
   ⓒ 책이에요.   ⓓ 책상이에요.

Track 058

9 ⓒ

10   A 가방이 누구 거예요?
   B ⓐ 마크 씨예요.   ⓑ 네, 맞아요.
     ⓒ 가방이에요.   ⓓ 마크 씨 거예요.

Track 059

10 ⓓ

► **Reading**

11 (1) 누구예요?   (2) 무슨 일 해요?

12 (1) 뭐예요?   (2) 누구 거예요?

Chapter 4   p.100

► **Grammar**

1 식당   2 병원   3 집에

4 약국에 있어요   5 어디에

6 어디에 있어요   7 위

8 왼쪽 / 옆   9 사이

► **Listening**

10   ⓐ 제인 씨가 식당에 있어요.
   ⓑ 제인 씨가 학교에 있어요.
   ⓒ 제인 씨가 은행에 있어요.
   ⓓ 제인 씨가 병원에 있어요.

Track 065

10 ⓒ

11   A 책이 어디에 있어요?
   B 책상 위에 있어요.
   A 책상 위 어디에 있어요?
   B 시계 옆에 있어요.

Track 066

11 ⓑ

► **Reading**

12 ⓒ

Chapter 5

p.110

▶ **Grammar**

1 ⓐ　　　2 ⓑ　　　3 ⓐ　　　4 ⓑ

5 한　　　6 두　　　7 다섯 잔

8 (1) 있어요　　　(2) 몇 개

9 (1) 있어요　　　(2) 몇 명 있어요

▶ **Listening**

Ex. 의자가 세 개 있어요.
10 동생이 네 명 있어요.
11 가방이 한 개 있어요.
12 표가 두 장 있어요.
13 책이 세 권 있어요.

Track 072

10 네　　　11 한　　　12 두　　　13 세

14 가방 안에 안경하고 지갑하고 휴지가 있어요. 그런데 우산이 없어요.
Track 073

14 ⓑ

▶ **Reading**

15 (1) 2　　(2) 0　　(3) 3　　(4) 0　　(5) 1

Chapter 6

p.120

▶ **Grammar**

1 육칠삼사에 오팔사이예요.
2 공일공에 사삼이팔에 구이육칠이에요.
3 이　　　　　　　4 시계가 아니에요
5 는　　　　　　　6 은

▶ **Listening**

7 A 병원 전화번호가 몇 번이에요?
　 B 794-5269예요.
8 A 유진 씨 핸드폰 번호가 몇 번이에요?
　 B 010-4539-8027이에요.
Track 079

7 ⓐ　　　　8 ⓒ

9 A 폴 씨, 혹시 제인 씨 집 전화번호 알아요?
　 B 아니요, 몰라요.
　　 그런데 제인 씨 핸드폰 번호는 알아요.
　 A 핸드폰 번호가 몇 번이에요?
　 B 010-7934-8205예요.
Track 080

9 ⓓ

▶ **Reading**

10 (1) ⓑ　　　　　　　(2) ⓐ

Chapter 7

p.130

▶ **Grammar**

1 칠월 십사일　　　2 시월 삼일
3 ⓑ　　　4 ⓐ　　　5 ⓑ
6 에　　　7 언제 / 무슨 요일에

▶ **Listening**

8-9 A 파티가 언제예요?
　　 B 8월 13일이에요.
　　 A 금요일이에요?
　　 B 아니요, 토요일이에요.
Track 086

8 ⓒ　　　　　　　9 ⓑ

▶ **Reading**

10 ⓐ　　　　　　　11 ⓓ

Chapter 8

p.140

▶ **Grammar**

1 한 시 삼십 분이에요. / 한 시 반이에요.
2 네 시 사십오 분이에요.
3 여섯 시 오십 분
4 세 시 이십 분에
5 부터, 까지
6 아홉 시부터 열두 시까지

7 5시 30분이에요.

8 2시 25분이에요.

9 7시 45분이에요.

Track **092**

7   8   9

10 A 인호 씨, 몇 시에 회사에 가요?
    B 10시에 가요.
    A 그럼, 몇 시에 은행에 가요?
    B 4시 20분에 가요.
    A 그럼, 언제 집에 가요?
    B 6시 반에 가요.

Track **093**

10 (1) 은행   (2) 10:00   (3) 6:30

▶ **Reading**

11 (1) 9:30   (2) 한국어 수업
    (3) 2:00   (4) 3:30~5:00
    (5) 집

Chapter 9   p.150

▶ **Grammar**

1 30분   2 1시간
3 2시간 40분
4 (1) 자동차로   (2) 45분
5 (1) 비행기로 가요   (2) 1시간 30분 걸려요
6 (1) 기차로 가요   (2) 3시간 걸려요

▶ **Listening**

7 ⓐ 비행기로 가요.
   ⓑ 자동차로 가요.
   ⓒ 자전거로 가요.
   ⓓ 버스로 가요.

8 ⓐ 배로 가요.
   ⓑ 지하철로 가요.
   ⓒ 기차로 가요.
   ⓓ 걸어서 가요.

Track **099**

---

9 ⓐ 집에서 회사까지 30분 걸려요.
   ⓑ 집에서 학교까지 30분 걸려요.
   ⓒ 집에서 회사까지 40분 걸려요.
   ⓓ 집에서 학교까지 40분 걸려요.

7 ⓑ   8 ⓓ   9 ⓓ

▶ **Reading**

10 ⓓ   11 ⓑ

Chapter 10   p.160

▶ **Grammar**

1 구천오백 원이에요
2 십만 삼천 원이에요
3 얼마
4 얼마예요
5 (1) 얼마예요   (2) 한
6 (1) 얼마예요   (2) 두 개 주세요

▶ **Listening**

7 A 커피가 얼마예요?
   B 6,700원이에요.

8 A 우산이 얼마예요?
   B 38,500원이에요.

Track **105**

7 ⓓ   8 ⓑ

9 A 뭐 드시겠어요?
   B 녹차 있어요?
   A 죄송합니다, 손님. 녹차가 없어요.
   B 그럼, 뭐 있어요?
   A 커피하고 주스 있어요.
   B 그럼, 커피 1잔 주세요. 얼마예요?
   A 4,500원입니다.
   B 돈 여기 있어요.

Track **106**

9 ⓒ

▶ **Reading**

10 O   11 X   12 X   13 X

▶ **Grammar**

1 ⓑ   2 ⓐ   3 (1) 에   (2) 에서
4 (1) 에   (2) 에서   5 (1) 에   (2) 에서
6 친구하고   7 혼자

▶ **Listening**

8 ⓐ 일해요.   ⓑ 식사해요.
   ⓒ 얘기해요.   ⓓ 여행해요.
9 ⓐ 노래해요.   ⓑ 운동해요.
   ⓒ 전화해요.   ⓓ 요리해요.

Track 112

8 ⓐ   9 ⓒ

10 A 누구하고 식사해요?
   B _____

Track 113

10 ⓒ

▶ **Reading**

11 X   12 X   13 O
14 O   15 X

▶ **Grammar**

1 ⓐ   2 ⓑ   3 ⓑ   4 ⓑ
5 (1) 끝나요   (2) 먹어요
  (3) 봐요   (4) 자요
6 (1) 가르쳐요   (2) 있어요
  (3) 만나요   (4) 마셔요
7 을   8 를   9 을   10 를

▶ **Listening**

11 폴 씨가 운동해요. 그다음에 샤워해요.
   그다음에 밥을 먹어요.
   그다음에 책을 읽어요.
Track 119

11 (4), (1), (3), (2)

▶ **Reading**

12 ⓑ → 식사를 해요(식사해요)
   ⓓ → 중국어
   ⓖ → 광주

▶ **Grammar**

1 ⓐ   2 ⓑ   3 ⓐ   4 ⓑ
5 안 바빠요   6 안 피곤해요
7 운동 안 해요   8 그래서
9 그런데   10 그리고

▶ **Listening**

11 제인이 일해요. 운동 안 해요.
   핸드폰을 봐요. 친구를 안 만나요.
   전화 안 해요. 공부해요.
   책을 안 읽어요. 음악을 들어요.

Track 125

11 핸드폰을 봐요, 공부해요, 음악을 들어요

12 ⓐ 바빠요.   ⓑ 길어요.
   ⓒ 멀어요.   ⓓ 추워요.
Track 126

12 ⓐ

▶ **Reading**

13 ⓐ   14 ⓒ   15 ⓑ

▶ **Grammar**

1 (1) 읽었어요   (2) 재미있었어요
2 (1) 했어요   (2) 많았어요
3 (1) 왔어요   (2) 배웠어요
4 7시간   5 일주일/7일 동안
6 3년 동안   7 산이, 바다
8 축구가

9 A 어제 제인 씨를 만났어요?
   B ⓐ 제인 씨가 어때요?
      ⓑ 아니요, 안 만났어요.
      ⓒ 네, 제인 씨가 아파요.
      ⓓ 제인 씨가 캐나다 사람이에요.

10 A 냉면하고 비빔밥 중에서 뭐가 더 좋아요?
   B ⓐ 냉면이 비싸요.
      ⓑ 식당에 가요.
      ⓒ 비빔밥이 없어요.
      ⓓ 비빔밥이 더 맛있어요.

Track 132

9 ⓑ   10 ⓓ

▶ Reading
11 ⓓ   12 ⓑ

Chapter 15   p.210

▶ Grammar
1 ⓑ   2 ⓐ   3 ⓐ   4 ⓑ
5 만날 거예요   6 읽을 거예요
7 볼 거예요   8 같이 영화 못 봐요
9 같이 술 못 마셔요

▶ Listening

10 내일 어디에 갈 거예요?
11 왜 같이 여행 못 가요?

Track 138

10 ⓐ   11 ⓒ

▶ Reading
12 ⓑ   13 ⓒ

Chapter 16   p.220

▶ Grammar
1 ⓐ   2 ⓐ   3 ⓑ
4 ⓑ   5 ⓑ   6 ⓑ   7 ⓑ
8 ⓐ   9 ⓑ

▶ Listening

10 ⓐ 일본 친구가 없어요.
    ⓑ 일본 친구가 많아요.
    ⓒ 일본 사람이 아니에요.
    ⓓ 일본어 얘기가 어려워요.

11 ⓐ 자동차가 있어요.
    ⓑ 운전할 수 있어요.
    ⓒ 자동차가 필요해요.
    ⓓ 운전을 배울 거예요.

Track 144

10 ⓑ   11 ⓓ

▶ Reading
12 ⓑ

Chapter 17   p.230

▶ Grammar
1 ⓓ 얘기해 주세요   2 ⓑ 빌려주세요
3 ⓐ 기다려 주세요
4 태권도요   5 시험요
6 못 들었어요   7 못 봤어요
8 못 들었어요   9 못 봤어요

▶ Listening

10 ⓐ 다시 들어 주세요.
    ⓑ 빨리 들어 주세요.
    ⓒ 천천히 말해 주세요.
    ⓓ 천천히 들어 주세요.

11 ⓐ 테니스를 배워 주세요.
    ⓑ 테니스를 가르쳐 주세요.
    ⓒ 테니스를 연습해 주세요.
    ⓓ 테니스 라켓을 빌려주세요.

12 ⓐ 핸드폰을 받아 주세요.
    ⓑ 전화번호를 말해 주세요.
    ⓒ 조금 전에 전화해 주세요.
    ⓓ 조금 후에 전화해 주세요.

Track 150

10 ⓒ   11 ⓑ   12 ⓓ

▶ Reading
13 (ⓑ) → (ⓐ) → (ⓓ) → (ⓒ)

Chapter 18

p.240

▶ **Grammar**

1 쉬고 싶어요   2   먹고 싶어요

3 얘기하고 싶어요

4 (1) 먹어 봤어요   (2) 먹어 보세요

5 (1) 입어 봤어요   (2) 입어 보세요

▶ **Listening**

> 6   김치가 맵지 않아요?
>
> 7   한국어 공부가 어렵지 않아요?
>
> Track **156**

6 ⓑ   7 ⓓ

▶ **Reading**

8 ⓓ   9 ⓑ

Chapter 19

p.250

▶ **Grammar**

1 (1) 걸으세요   (2) 드세요/잡수세요

2 (1) 마시지 마세요   (2) 피우지 마세요

3 (1) 없습니다   (2) 먹습니다

    (3) 마십니다   (4) 봅니다

4 ⓐ   5   ⓑ

▶ **Listening**

> 6-7 A   명동에 가 주세요.
>   B   명동 어디요?
>   A   저기 신호등에서 오른쪽으로 가세요.
>   B   그다음은요?
>   A   병원에서 왼쪽으로 가세요.
>   그리고 은행 앞에서 세워 주세요.
>   B   네, 알겠습니다.
>   A   얼마예요?
>   B   7,400원입니다.
>   A   여기 있어요. 수고하세요.
>   B   감사합니다. 안녕히 가세요.
>
> Track **162**

6 ⓒ   7 ⓑ

▶ **Reading**

8 ⓒ   9 ⓐ

Chapter 20

p.260

▶ **Grammar**

1 (1) 가세요   (2) 좋아하셨어요

    (3) 좋아하세요   (4) 드셨어요/잡수셨어요

    (5) 드세요/잡수세요   (6) 주무셨어요

    (7) 주무세요

2 (1) ⓐ   (2) ⓑ

3 (1) ⓐ   (2) ⓑ

4 배우세요

5 어려우세요

6 드셨어요

▶ **Listening**

> 7-8 A   신촌 식당입니다.
>   B   저, 예약돼요?
>   A   네, 됩니다. 언제 오실 거예요?
>   B   오늘 저녁 7시에 갈 거예요.
>   A   몇 명 오실 거예요?
>   B   3명요.
>   A   성함이 어떻게 되세요?
>   B   제인 브라운입니다.
>   A   연락처가 어떻게 되세요?
>   B   010-3780-9254입니다.
>   A   예약됐습니다. 6시 50분까지 오세요.
>   B   네, 알겠어요.
>
> Track **168**

7 ⓑ   8 ⓓ

▶ **Reading**

9 ⓓ

Glossary of Words

[A]

a bit ·············· 좀 ·············· 186
a cold ·············· 감기 ·············· 187
a little ·············· 좀 ·············· 186
a little while ago ·············· 아까 ·············· 138
a little while later ·············· 이따가 ·············· 138
a lot ·············· 많이 ·············· 187
(to be) a lot ·············· 많다 ·············· 186
a particular thing ·············· 별일 ·············· 206
(to feel) afraid ·············· 무섭다 ·············· 258
Africa ·············· 아프리카 ·············· 68
after that ·············· 그다음에 ·············· 166
afternoon ·············· 오후 ·············· 137
again ·············· 또, 다시 ·············· 67,226
athlete ·············· 운동선수 ·············· 78
air conditioner ·············· 에어컨 ·············· 118
airport ·············· 공항 ·············· 98
all together ·············· 모두, 전부 ·············· 107, 156
also ·············· 도 ·············· 107, 238
America ·············· 아메리카 ·············· 68
American ·············· 미국 사람 ·············· 67
and (used between nouns) ····· 하고 ·············· 107
and (used between sentences)
·············· 그리고 ·············· 187
(to feel) angry ·············· 화가 나다 ·············· 258
another ·············· 다른 ·············· 217
(to) answer ·············· 대답하다 ·············· 198
appointment ·············· 약속 ·············· 217
Argentina ·············· 아르헨티나 ·············· 68
arms ·············· 팔 ·············· 188
around ·············· 쯤 ·············· 137
(to) arrive ·············· 도착하다 ·············· 168, 227
Asia ·············· 아시아 ·············· 68
(to) ask ·············· 물어보다 ·············· 198
Australia ·············· 호주 ·············· 68
(to be) available ·············· 되다 ·············· 256

[B]

(to be) bad ·············· 나쁘다, 못하다 ·············· 208, 216
(to feel) bad ·············· 기분이 나쁘다 ·············· 258
bank ·············· 은행 ·············· 98
(to feel) bashful ·············· 부끄럽다 ·············· 258
basketball ·············· 농구 ·············· 218
bathroom ·············· 화장실 ·············· 96
(to) be ·············· 있다 ·············· 207

(to be) beautiful ·············· 아름답다 ·············· 197, 238
before ·············· 전에 ·············· 138
(to) begin ·············· 시작하다 ·············· 236
behind ·············· 뒤 ·············· 97
belly ·············· 배 ·············· 188
beside ·············· 옆 ·············· 96
best ·············· 제일 ·············· 197
bicycle ·············· 자전거 ·············· 148, 218
(to be) big ·············· 크다 ·············· 208
bill ·············· 지폐 ·············· 158
birthday ·············· 생일 ·············· 126
(to be) blocked ·············· 막히다 ·············· 227
boat ·············· 배 ·············· 148
book ·············· 책 ·············· 87
bookstore ·············· 서점 ·············· 98
(to be) bored ·············· 심심하다 ·············· 238
(to be) boring ·············· 재미없다 ·············· 208
(to) borrow ·············· 빌리다 ·············· 178
Brazil ·············· 브라질 ·············· 68
bread ·············· 빵 ·············· 156
breakfast ·············· 아침 (식사) ·············· 138
bridge ·············· 다리 ·············· 248
(to be) bright ·············· 밝다 ·············· 208
bus ·············· 버스 ·············· 147, 148
bus stop ·············· 버스 정류장 ·············· 248
Busan (a large city in the south)
·············· 부산 ·············· 157
business card ·············· 명함 ·············· 88
business trip ·············· 출장 ·············· 207
(to be) busy ·············· 바쁘다 ·············· 238
but ·············· 그런데 ·············· 117, 237
(to) buy a book ·············· 책을 사다 ·············· 178
by (a time) ·············· 까지 ·············· 257
by any chance ·············· 혹시 ·············· 116
by the way ·············· 그런데 ·············· 237

[C]

café ·············· 카페 ·············· 98
cafe latte ·············· 카페라테 ·············· 156
(to) call ·············· 전화하다 ·············· 168
Canada ·············· 캐나다 ·············· 68
cannot ·············· 못 ·············· 207
car ·············· 자동차 ·············· 148
(to be) careful ·············· 조심하다 ·············· 186
cash card ·············· 현금카드 ·············· 158

casual expression for a man over thirty
아저씨 246
(to) catch a cold 감기에 걸리다 187
cell phone 핸드폰 88
(to) chat 얘기하다 198
(to be) cheap 싸다 208
chest 가슴 188
China 중국 68
(to) choose 선택하다 198
Chuseok (Korean Thanksgiving)
추석 127
class 수업 137
(to be) clean 깨끗하다 208
(it is) close 가까워요 146
coin 동전 158
(to be) cold 춥다 187, 208
comb 빗 88
(I) come 와요 136
company 회사 98, 117
(to be) complicated 복잡하다 238
computer 컴퓨터 118
contact information (phone number)
연락처 256
contrast marker 은/는 117
convenience store 편의점 98, 246
(to be) convenient 편리하다 238
(to) cook 요리하다 168
cooking 요리 177
corner 모퉁이 248
cough 기침 187
counter for people 명 107
counting word for people [honorific]
분 256
counting word for tickets 장 157
counting work for time frequency
번 168
country 나라 67
cousin 사촌 108
co-worker 동료 166
credit card 신용카드 158
(to) cross 건너다 248
crosswalk 횡단보도 248
(to) cry 울다 198

[D]
(to be) dark 어둡다 208
daughter 딸 108
day 일 126
(to) depart 출발하다 168
department store 백화점 97

different 다른 217
(to be) different 다르다 208
(to be) difficult 어렵다 208, 236
(to be) difficult (situation) 힘들다 238
dinner 저녁 (식사) 138
(to be) dirty 더럽다 208
(I) do 해요 77
(to) do 하다 218
doctor 의사 78
door 문 228
double room 2인실 257
(to) drink 마시다 197
(to) drink coffee 커피를 마시다 178
(to) dirve 운전하다 168
driver's license 운전면허증 88

[E]
each 마다 176
(to be) easy 쉽다 208
early 일찍 136
ears 귀 188
(I) eat 식사해요 126
(to) eat food 음식을 먹다 178
elevator 엘리베이터 228
(to feel) embarrassed 당황하다 258
embassy 대사관 98
emergency exit 비상구 228
English 영어 77
Europe 유럽 68
evening 저녁 136
every 마다 176
every day 매일 136
every week 매주 176
(to) exercise 운동하다 168
exit 출구 226
(to be) expensive 비싸다 208
eye 눈 188

[F]
fax 팩스 118
family 가족 107
famous 유명하다 237
fan 선풍기 118
(it is) far 멀어요 146
(to be) far 멀다 208
(to be) fat 뚱뚱하다 208
father 아버지 108
(to be) few 적다 208
film 영화 176

(to) find	찾다	198, 237
(to be) fine	괜찮다	216
finger	손가락	188
(to) finish	끝나다	178
fire extinguisher	소화기	228
five (the native Korean number)		
	다섯	107
food	음식	177
foot	발	188
for (time duration)	동안	196
foreginer's registration card		
	외국인 등록증	88
(to) forget	잊어버리다	198
four-way intersection	사거리	248
France	프랑스	68
frequently	자주	168
Friday	금요일	126
friend	친구	87, 177
(to be) friendly	친절하다	238
from	한테서	177
from (place)	에서	146
from (time)	부터	137
from here	여기에서	146
from whom	누구한테서	177
front	앞	168
frost	서리	238
(to be) full	배부르다	208
(to be) fun	재미있다	177, 208

[G]

Gangnam	강남	226
garbage can	휴지통	228
gas station	주유소	98
Germany	독일	68
(to) get along	지내다	236
(to) get off	내리다	248
(to) get on	타다	248
(to) get ready	준비하다	168
(to) get up	일어나다	178
Ghana	가나	68
(to) give a present	선물을 주다	198
Give me (noun)	주세요	156
glasses	안경	88
(I) go	가요	136
(to) go and return	다녀오다	207
(to) go hiking in the mountains		
	등산하다	168
(to) go on a business trip	출장 가다	207
(to) go on a date	데이트하다	168
go on a trip	여행가다	237

(to) go on a trip	여행하다	196
(to) go straight	직진하다	247
(to feel) good	기분이 좋다	258
(to be) good	좋다	197, 208
grandfather	할아버지	108
grandmother	할머니	108
Great Britain	영국	68
Gwanghwamun (area of Seoul)		
	광화문	246
gym	헬스장	98

[H]

hair	머리카락	188
half hour	반	136
hall	복도	228
(to feel) happy	행복하다	258
(I) have	있어요	106
(to) have a cough	기침이 나다	187
(to) have a meal	식사하다	166, 168
(to) have dinner	저녁 식사하다	166
(to) have meeting	회의하다	168
hand	손	188
head	머리	187, 188
health	건강	186
(to be) healthy	건강하다	238
(to) hear	듣다	226
(to be) heavy	무겁다	208
(to) help	도와주다	178
here	여기	106
here and there	여기저기	196
(to) hit	치다	218
home	집	117
hospital	병원	98
(to be) hot	덥다	208
hour (time duration)	시간	146
hour (time)	시	136
house	집	97, 98
housewife	주부	78
how	어떻게	147
How about...?	(은/는) 어때요?	176
how long	얼마나, 얼마 동안	146, 196
how many	몇	106
how many days	며칠 동안	257
how many people〔honorific〕		
	몇 분	256
how much	얼마나	156
however	그런데	117
(to be) hungry	배고프다	208
(to) hurt	아프다	186
husband	남편	108

[I]

I	나, 저는, 제가	66, 108, 216
I don't know	몰라요	97
I know	알아요	97
in total (referring only to people)	모두, 전부	107, 156
(to be) inconvenient	불편하다	238
India	인도	68
indicating the arrival city	행	157
Indonesia	인도네시아	68
Insadong (area of Seoul)	인사동	197
(to be) interesting	재미있다	177, 208
interpreter	통역사	78
iron	다리미	118
it takes (time)	걸려요	146
Italy	이탈리아	68

[J]

Japan	일본	68, 207
Jeju Island	제주도	196
just	바로, 만, 그냥	97, 168, 186

[K]

key	열쇠	88
knee	무릎	188
Korea	한국	67, 68
Korea Train Express (super high-speed train)	KTX	157
Korean	한국 사람	67
Korean	한국어	87

[L]

laptop	노트북	118
last month	지난달	128
last week	지난주	128
last year	작년	128
later	나중에	138, 176
(to) laugh	웃다	198
lawyer	변호사	78
(to) learn	배우다	177
(to) learn Korean	한국어를 배우다	198
(to) leave	떠나다	198
legs	다리미	188
(to be) light	가볍다	208
(to) like	좋아하다	176
(to) listen to	듣다	226
(to) listen to music	음악을 듣다	178
(to) live	살다	178
(to) lodge	묵다	257
(to be) long	길다	208
(to) look around	구경하다	196
(to) look for	찾다	198
(to) lose	잃어버리다	198
(to be) loud	시끄럽다	208
lower back	허리	188
lunar calendar	음력	127
lunch	점심 (식사)	138

[M]

(to) make	만들다	177, 178
(to) make a reservation	예약하다	257
Malaysia	말레이시아	68
(to be) many	많다	208
market	시장	98
maternal aunt	이모	108
maternal uncle	외삼촌	108
me too	저도	176
meal	밥	86
(to) meet friend(s)	친구를 만나다	178
(to) meet friend(s)	만나다	226
Mexico	멕시코	68
microwave	전자레인지	118
military personnel	군인	78
minute	분	136
mirror	거울	88
Miss	씨	67
Mokdong (area of Seoul)	목동	146
money	돈	247
monk	스님	78
month	월	126
more	더	238
morning	아침	136
morning [formal]	오전	157
most	제일	197
mother	어머니	108
mountain	산	237
mouth	입	188
(to) move (to a new home)	이사하다	168
movie	영화	176
movie theater	영화관	98
movie ticket	영화표	217
Mr.	씨	67
Mrs.	씨	67
Mugunghwa Express (public passenger train)	무궁화호	157
my	제	87
my house	우리 집	206
my wife	아내	108

Myeongdong (area in Seoul) · 명동 ················· 247

[N]

name ·························· 이름 ················· 66
name [honorific] ············· 성함 ················· 256
Namsan (famous mountain in Seoul)
 ····························· 남산 ················· 197
(to be) near ················· 가깝다 ················ 208
neck ························· 목 ·················· 188
negation of verb ············· 안 ·················· 186
New Zealand ················ 뉴질랜드 ··············· 68
next month ·················· 다음 달 ··············· 128
next time ···················· 다음에 ················ 67
next week ··················· 다음 주 ·········· 128, 207
next weekend ················ 다음 주말에 ············· 257
next year ···················· 내년 ················· 128
nose ························ 코 ·················· 188
now ························· 지금 ············· 136, 138
number ····················· 번 ·················· 116
nun ························· 수녀(님) ··············· 78
nurse ························ 간호사 ················ 78

[O]

Oceania ···················· 오세아니아 ·············· 68
office worker ················· 회사원 ·········· 76, 78, 117
often ························ 자주 ················· 168
(to be) OK ·················· 괜찮다 ················ 238
(to be) okay ················· 괜찮다 ················ 216
older brother (of a man) ······· 형 ·············· 107, 108
older brother (of a woman) ····· 오빠 ················· 108
older sister (of a man) ········· 누나 ················· 108
older sister (of a woman) ······· 언니 ················· 108
on foot ····················· 걸어서 ··········· 146, 148
once ························ 한번 ················· 177
once more ·················· 다시 한번 ·············· 226
one ························· 하나 ················· 156
one week ··················· 일주일 ················ 168
one year ···················· 1년 ················· 168
only ························ 만 ·················· 168
or ·························· (이)나 ················ 237
order ······················ 주문 ················· 156
our ························· 우리 ················· 206
over there ··················· 저기 ················· 96

[P]

parents ····················· 부모님 ················ 107
park ························ 공원 ·············· 98, 168
parking lot ·················· 주차장 ················ 98

(to) pass by ················· 지나다 ················ 248
(to) pass time ················ 지내다 ················ 236
passport ···················· 여권 ················· 88
pastor ······················ 목사(님) ··············· 78
paternal aunt ················· 고모 ················· 108
paternal uncle ················ 삼촌 ················· 108
pedestrian bridge ············· 육교 ················· 248
per ························· 에 ·················· 168
person ····················· 사람 ················· 67
pharmacy ··················· 약국 ·············· 97, 98
Philippines ·················· 필리핀 ················ 68
phone ······················ 전화(기) ·············· 118
phone number ··············· 전화번호 ·············· 116
photo ······················ 사진 ················· 88
piano ······················ 피아노 ················ 218
plane ······················ 비행기 ················ 148
(to) play ···················· 놀다 ················· 178
(to) play tennis ··············· 테니스(를) 치다 ········· 216
policeman ··················· 경찰 ················· 78
(to be) poor ················· 못하다 ················ 216
(to be) possible ··············· 되다 ················· 256
post office ··················· 우체국 ··········· 98, 246
(to) practice ················· 연습하다 ·············· 168
(to) prepare ················· 준비하다 ·············· 168
(to be) pretty ················· 예쁘다 ················ 238
priest ······················ 신부(님) ··············· 78
professor ··················· 교수(님) ··············· 78
(to) put on clothes ············ 옷을 입다 ·············· 198
(to) put on shoes ············· 신발을 신다 ············· 198

[Q]
(to be) quiet ················· 조용하다 ·············· 208

[R]
(to) read a book ·············· 책을 읽다 ·············· 178
(to) receive ·················· 받다 ················· 198
really ······················ 정말 ················· 147
(to be) refreshing ············· 시원하다 ·············· 238
refrigerator ·················· 냉장고 ················ 118
relatives ···················· 친척 ················· 108
(to) reply ··················· 대답하다 ·············· 198
(to) rest ···················· 쉬다 ················· 178
resevation ··················· 예약 ················· 256
restaurant ··················· 식당 ·············· 98, 166
rice ························ 밥 ·················· 86
(to) ride ···················· 타다 ············· 218, 248
right ······················· 바로 ················· 97
right side ··················· 오른쪽 ················ 247
road ······················· 길 ·················· 227

| room | 방 | 257 |
| Russia | 러시아 | 68 |

[S]

(to feel) sad	슬프다	258
(to be) salty	짜다	238
Saturday	토요일	217
scenery	경치	197
school	학교	137
sea	바다	237
seafood	해산물	237
(I) see	봐요	67
(to) see	보다	176
(to) sell	팔다	178
Seoul (South Korea's capital city)	서울	157
ship	배	148
(to) shop	쇼핑하다	168
(to be) short	키가 작다	208
(to be) short	짧다	208
shoulders	어깨	188
(to feel) sick	아프다	258
(to be) simple	간단하다	238
Sinchon (area of Seoul)	신촌	97
(to) sing	노래하다	168
Singapore	싱가포르	68
skate	스케이트	218
ski	스키	218
(to be) skinny	마르다	208
(to) sleep	자다	178
(to feel) sleepy	졸리다	258
(to be) small	작다	208
so	그래서, 그러니까	177, 187
so (if so)	그럼	76
soccer	축구	218
someone's wife	부인	108
something	일	207
something else	또	197
son	아들	108
sound	소리	238
South Africa	남아프리카 공화국	68
Spain	스페인	68
(to) speak	말하다	178, 226
speaker	스피커	118
(to be) spicy	맵다	238
spoon	숟가락	86
stairs	계단	228
(to) start	시작하다	168, 236
(to) stay	있다, 묵다	207, 257
still	아직	237
(to) stop	세우다	246
store	가게	98
student	학생	76, 78
(to) study	공부하다	168
(to be) stylish	멋있다	238
subway	지하철	146, 148
subway or train station	지하철역	226
subway station	지하철역	248
Sunday	일요일	176
(to feel) surprised	놀라다	258
(to be) sweet	달다	238
(to) swim	수영하다	216

[T]

table tennis	탁구	218
(to) talk	얘기하다	168
(to be) tall	키가 크다	208
taekwondo	태권도	218
Taiwan	대만	68
(to be) tasty	맛있다	238
(to) take a picture	사진을 찍다	198
taxi driver	택시 기사	78, 148
(to) teach	가르쳐 주다	216
(to) teach English	영어를 가르치다	198
teacher	선생님	76, 78
teeth	이	188
television	텔레비전	118
tennis	테니스	216, 218
Thailand	태국	68
(to) thank (someone)	수고하다	247
that	저게	86
that day	그때	126
the ladies' room	여자 화장실	228
the marker for destination	에	136
the marker for means of transportation	(으)로	146
the marker for the direction in the meaning of "to"	으로	247
the marker in the meaning of "until, up to"	까지	247
the men's room	남자 화장실	228
the object marker	을/를	176
the place marker with action verbs	에서	166
(to be) the same	같다	208
the time marker	에어컨	126
there	거기	207
then	그럼, 그때	76, 126
there is	있어요	96
therefore	그래서, 그러니까	177, 187

these days	요즘	177
thing	거	87
(to) think	생각하다	198
this	이게, 이	86, 96
this month	이번 달	128
this time	이번	196
this week	이번 주	126, 128
this year	올해	128
Thursday	목요일	207
ticket	표	157
time	시간	126, 147
(to be, feel) tired	피곤하다	186, 258
tissue	휴지	88
to (place)	까지	146
to (time)	까지	137
today	오늘	128, 136
toe	발가락	188
together	같이	126
tomorrow	내일	128, 206
too (much)	너무	147
too much (many)	너무 많이	227
toothbrush	칫솔	88
toothpaste	치약	88
(to be) tough	힘들다	238
traditional tea	전통차	197
traffic light	신호등	247, 248
train	기차	148, 157
translator	번역가	78
travel	여행	196
(to) travel	여행하다	168
travel destination	여행지	237
trip	여행	196
two	두	106
two or three times	두세 번	168

[U]

U.S.A.	미국	67, 68
umbrella	우산	88, 106
(to be) uncomfortable	불편하다	238
(to be) uninteresting	재미없다	208
unit counter	개	106
usually	보통	136
(to) use	사용하다	198
(to) use a computer	컴퓨터하다	168

[V]

vacuum cleaner	청소기	118
vending machine	자판기	96, 228
vicinity	근처	96

| Vietnam | 베트남 | 68 |

[W]

waist	허리	188
(to) wait	기다리다	227
(to) wait for friends	친구를 기다리다	198
(I) wake up	일어나요	147
washing machine	세탁기	118
watch	시계	88
(to) watch a movie	영화를 보다	178
water	물	86
water purifier	정수기	118, 228
weather	날씨	187
weekend	주말	257
well	잘	207
what	뭐, 몇, 무슨	66, 116, 207
what day	며칠	126
what kind of	무슨	77
what number	몇 번	116
what time	몇 시에	136
when	언제	126
where	어디에, 어디에서	96, 166
which	어느	67
who	누구	87
whose	누구	87
why	왜	147
window	창문	228
with whom	누구하고	166
won (Korean currency)	원	156
(to) work	일하다	166, 168
work	일	77, 136
(to) worry	걱정하다	198
(to) write	쓰다	178

[Y]

yesterday	어제	128, 197
younger sibling	동생	107
younger brother	남동생	108
younger sister	여동생	108